© 2016 Live on Camera Media Group

All rights reserved. No part of this publication may be reproduced, distributed or transmitted in any form or by any means, including photocopying, recording, or other electronic or mechanical methods, without the prior written permission of the publisher, except in the case of brief quotations embodied in critical reviews and certain other noncommercial uses permitted by copyright law.

Over the Edge Books, Los Angeles

www.overtheedgebooks.com

Naked Art: An Expose in Bodypainting/Live on Camera Media Group—1st ed.
ISBN 978-1-944082-13-0

Naked Art
An Expose in Bodypainting

Born and raised in San Paolo, a city with many similarities to New York, was likely a contributing factor to the artistic personality that evolved into Binho Ribeiro. His journey started in Brazil, then went on to other South American countries. Countries like Chile and Argentina showed their interest for the new art style and from these travels the path of the graffiti writer Bino Ribeiro began to strengthen and take shape. The 2000's ushered in the begining of a new era. During this period an opportunity came about for Binho to work in Japan as a "Dekasequi", taking Binho to the other side of the world, but the environment and mentalities weren't an ideal place for the restless graffiti artist. However this traveling stirred Binho's soul and he went on a hunt for his tribe and a quest to find what his artistic soul was searching for: a way to express his ideas through his art. This urge wasn't appreciated by the modern but strict Tokyo Metropoli. So after one year of living in Japan, Binho took his new artistic references and returned to Brazil to start a new period of concepts and challenges.

BINHO

WWW.BINHORIBEIRO.COM.BR

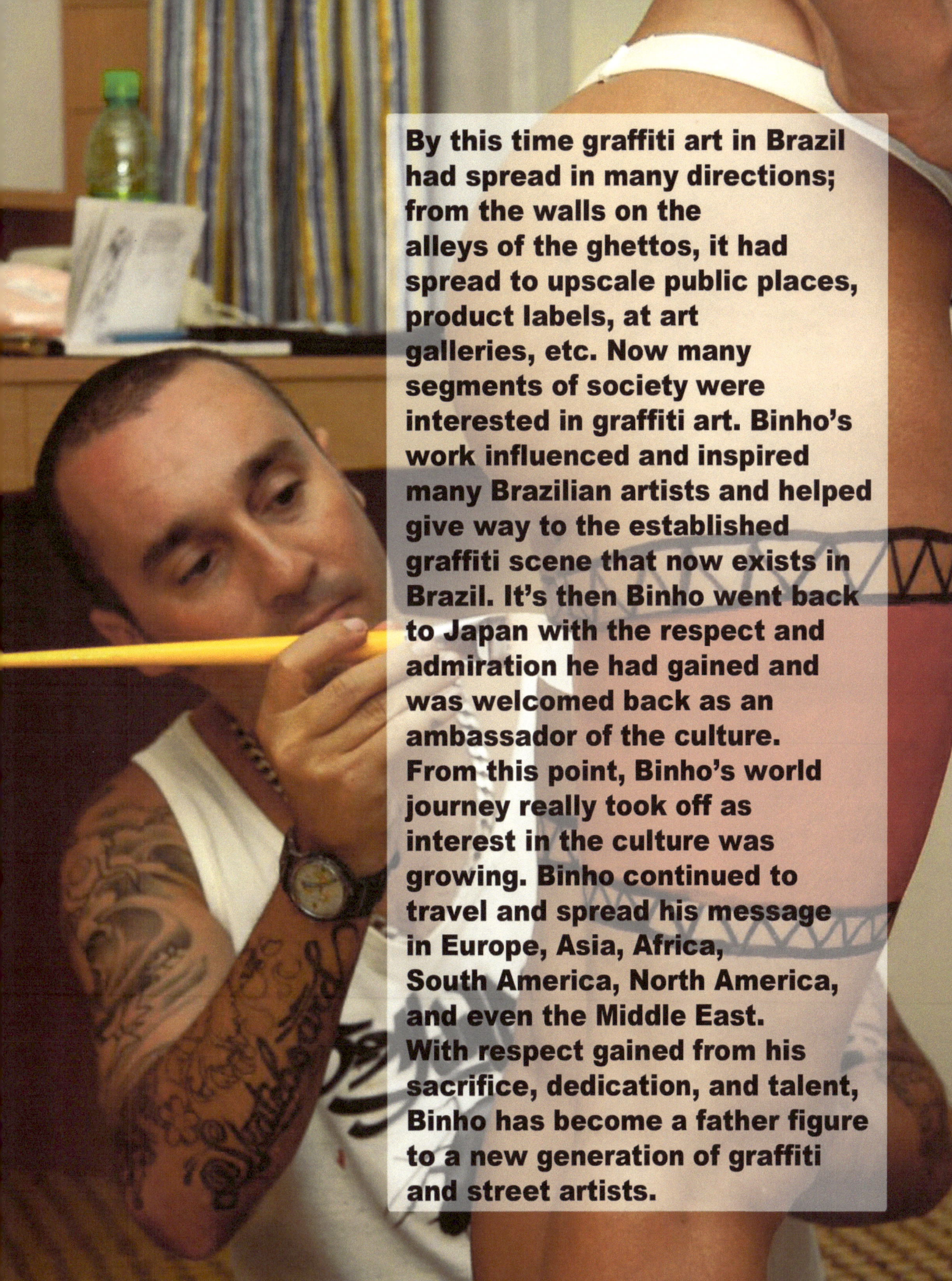

By this time graffiti art in Brazil had spread in many directions; from the walls on the alleys of the ghettos, it had spread to upscale public places, product labels, at art galleries, etc. Now many segments of society were interested in graffiti art. Binho's work influenced and inspired many Brazilian artists and helped give way to the established graffiti scene that now exists in Brazil. It's then Binho went back to Japan with the respect and admiration he had gained and was welcomed back as an ambassador of the culture. From this point, Binho's world journey really took off as interest in the culture was growing. Binho continued to travel and spread his message in Europe, Asia, Africa, South America, North America, and even the Middle East. With respect gained from his sacrifice, dedication, and talent, Binho has become a father figure to a new generation of graffiti and street artists.

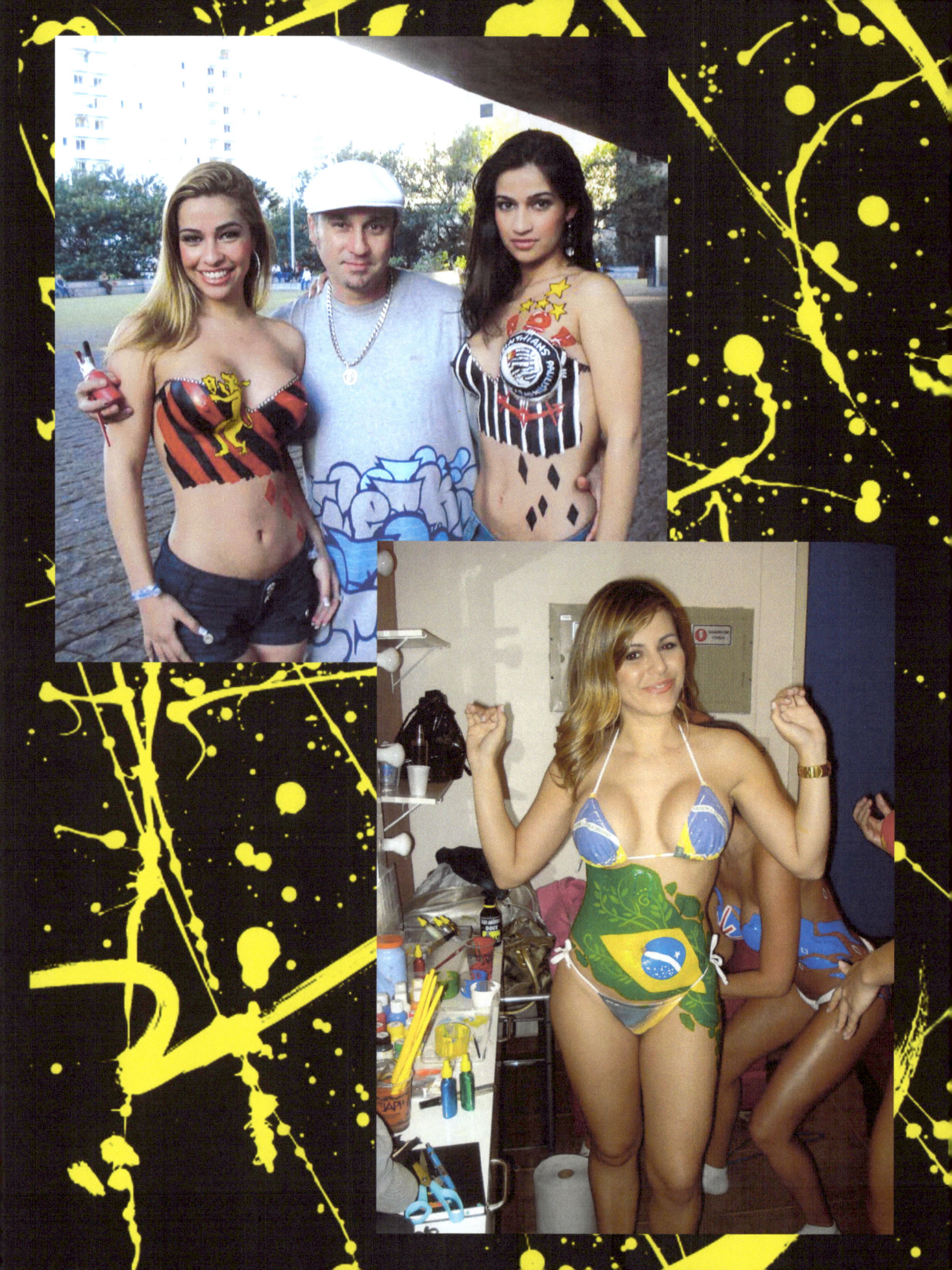

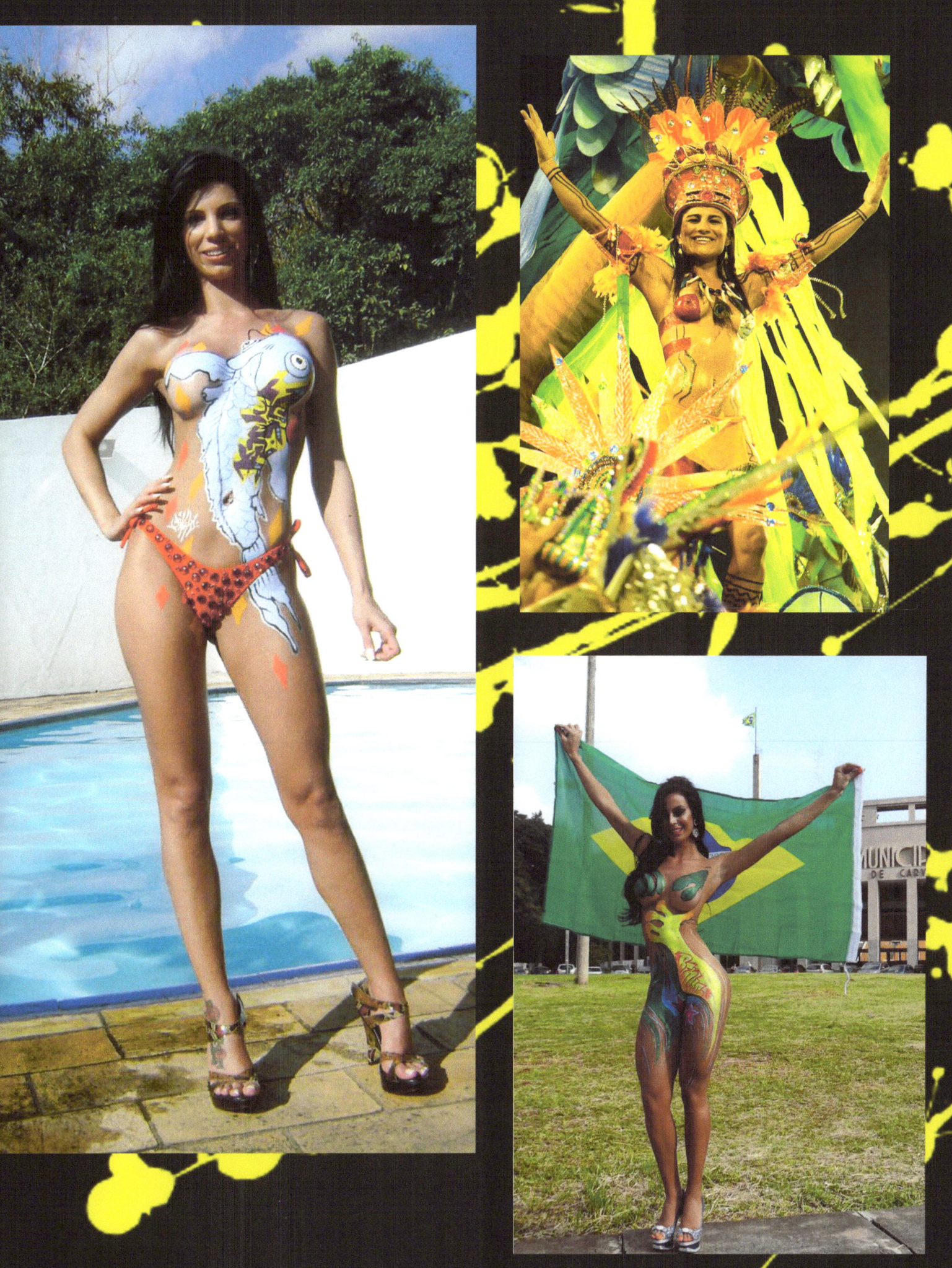

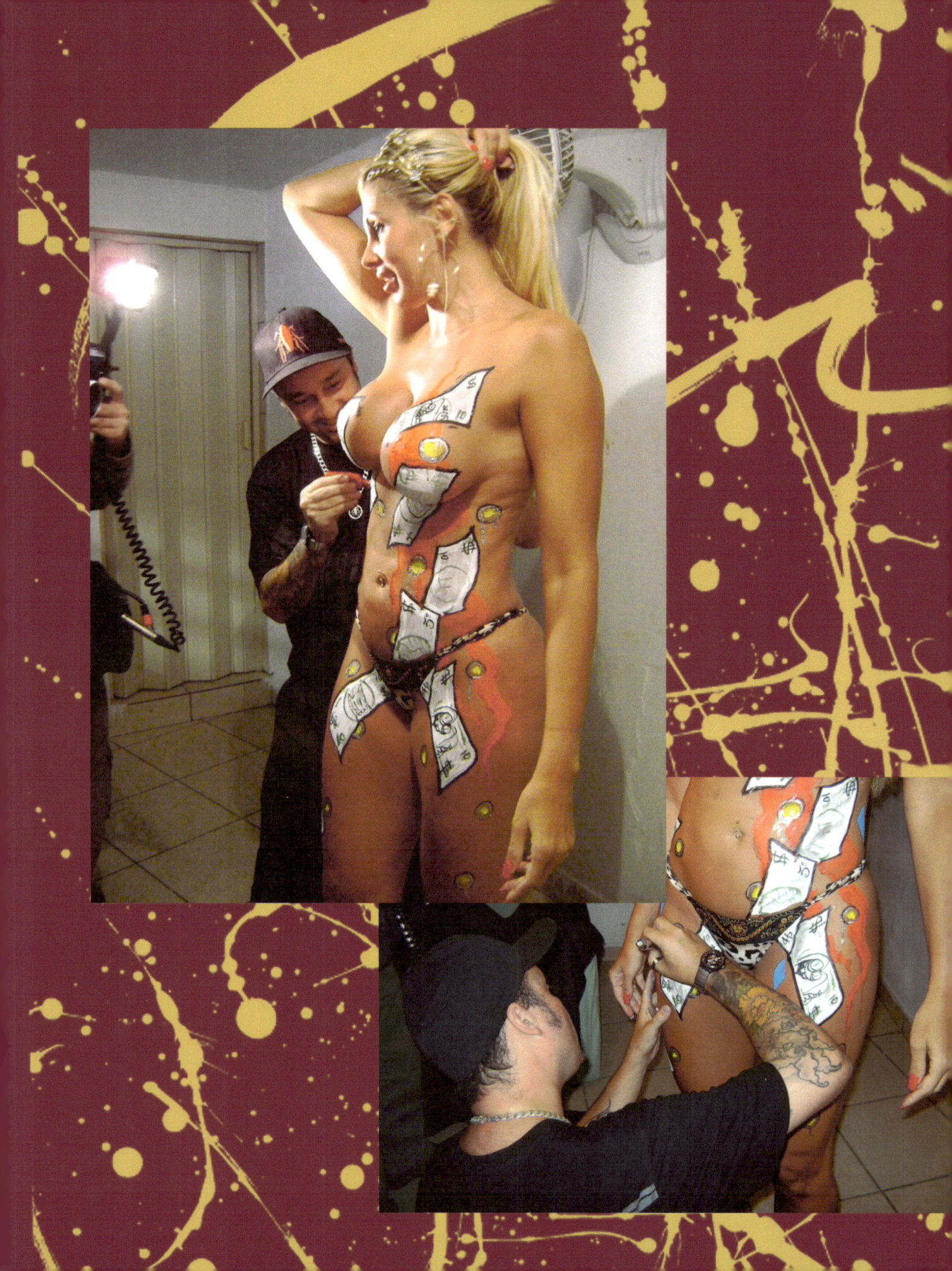

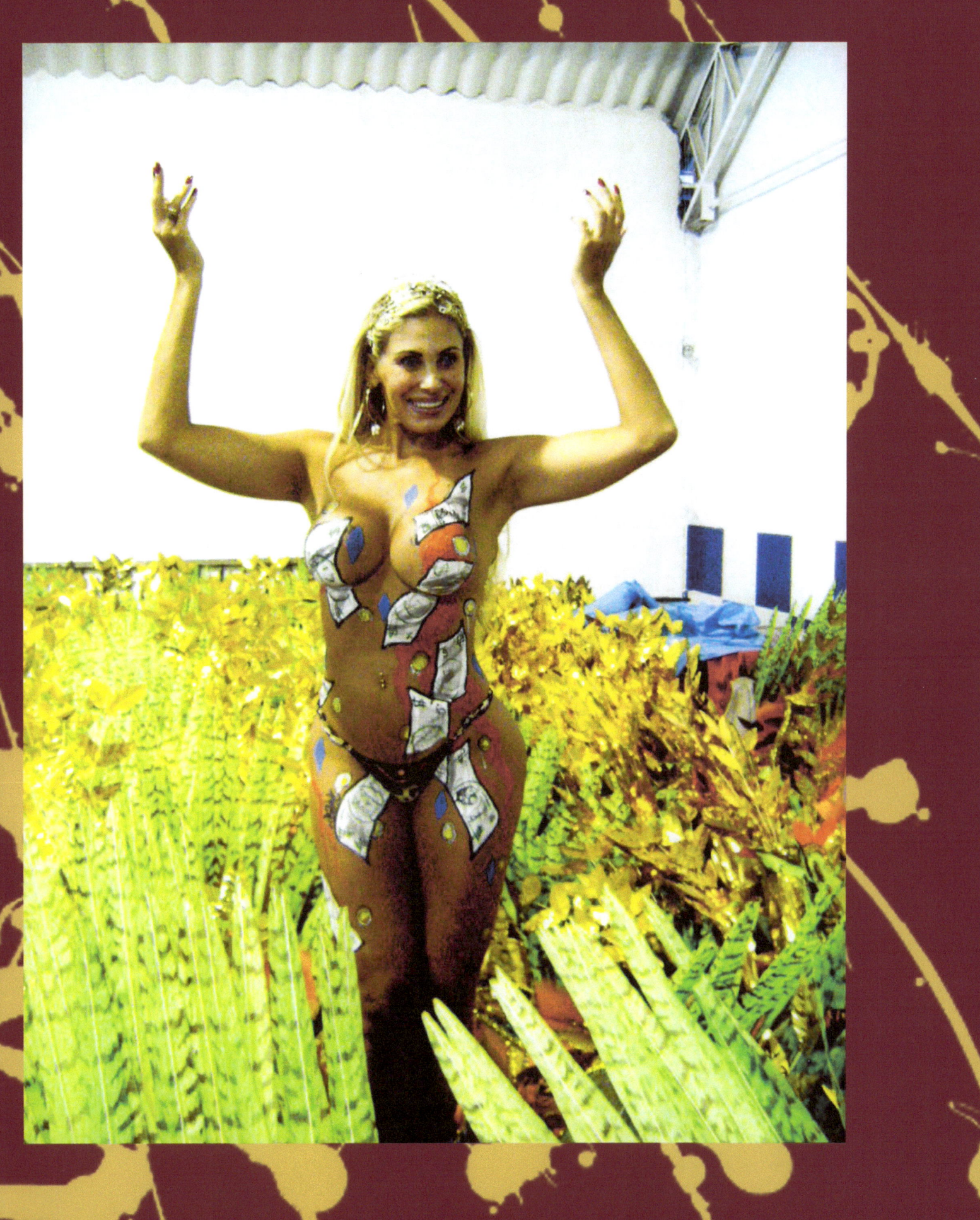

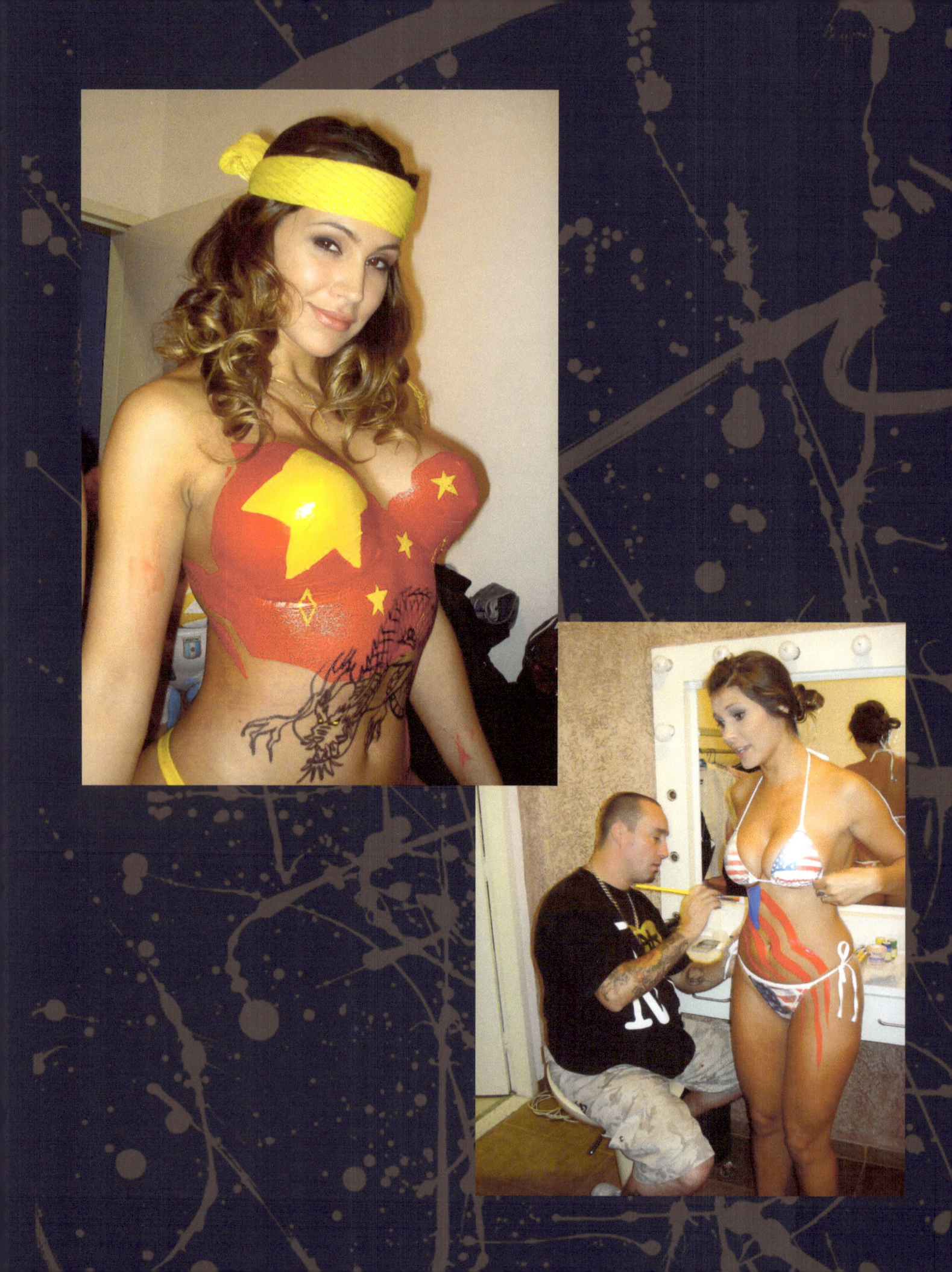

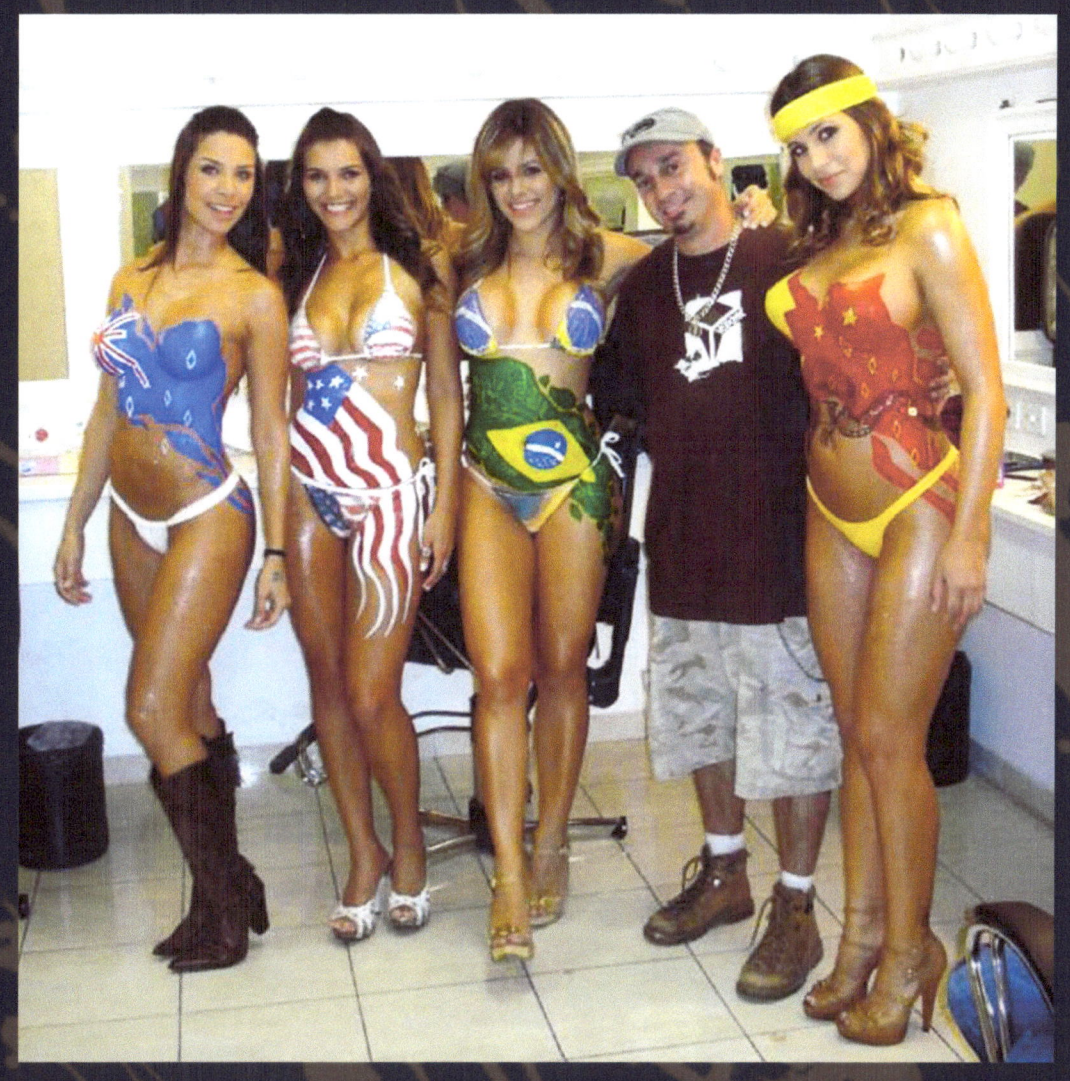
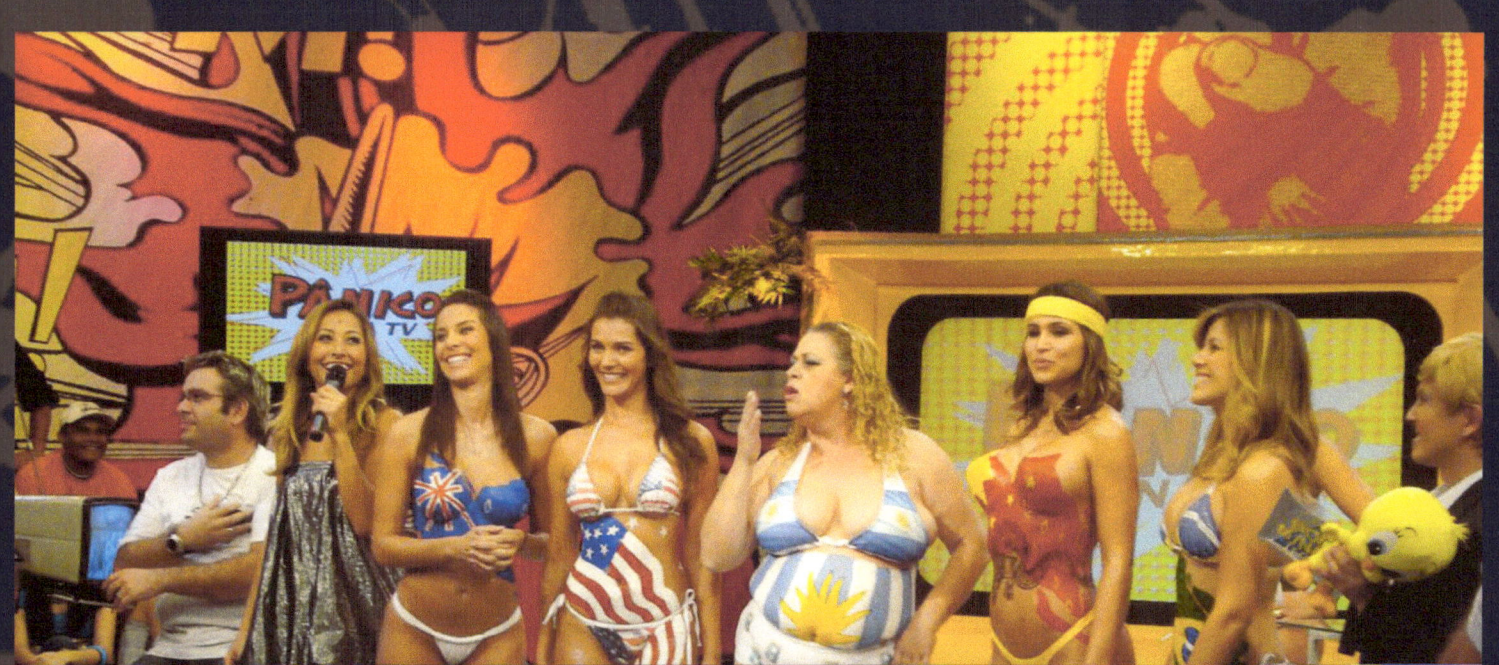

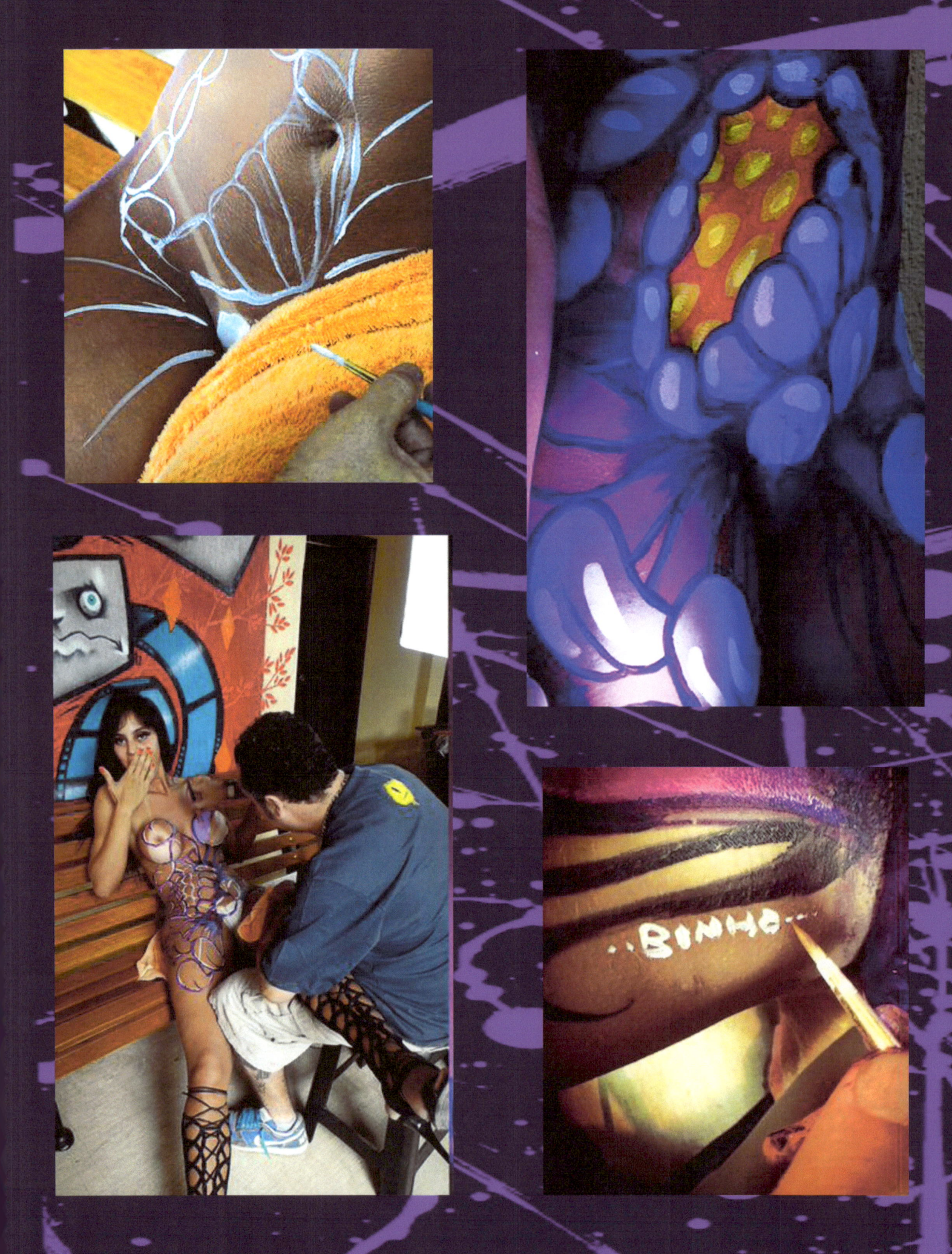

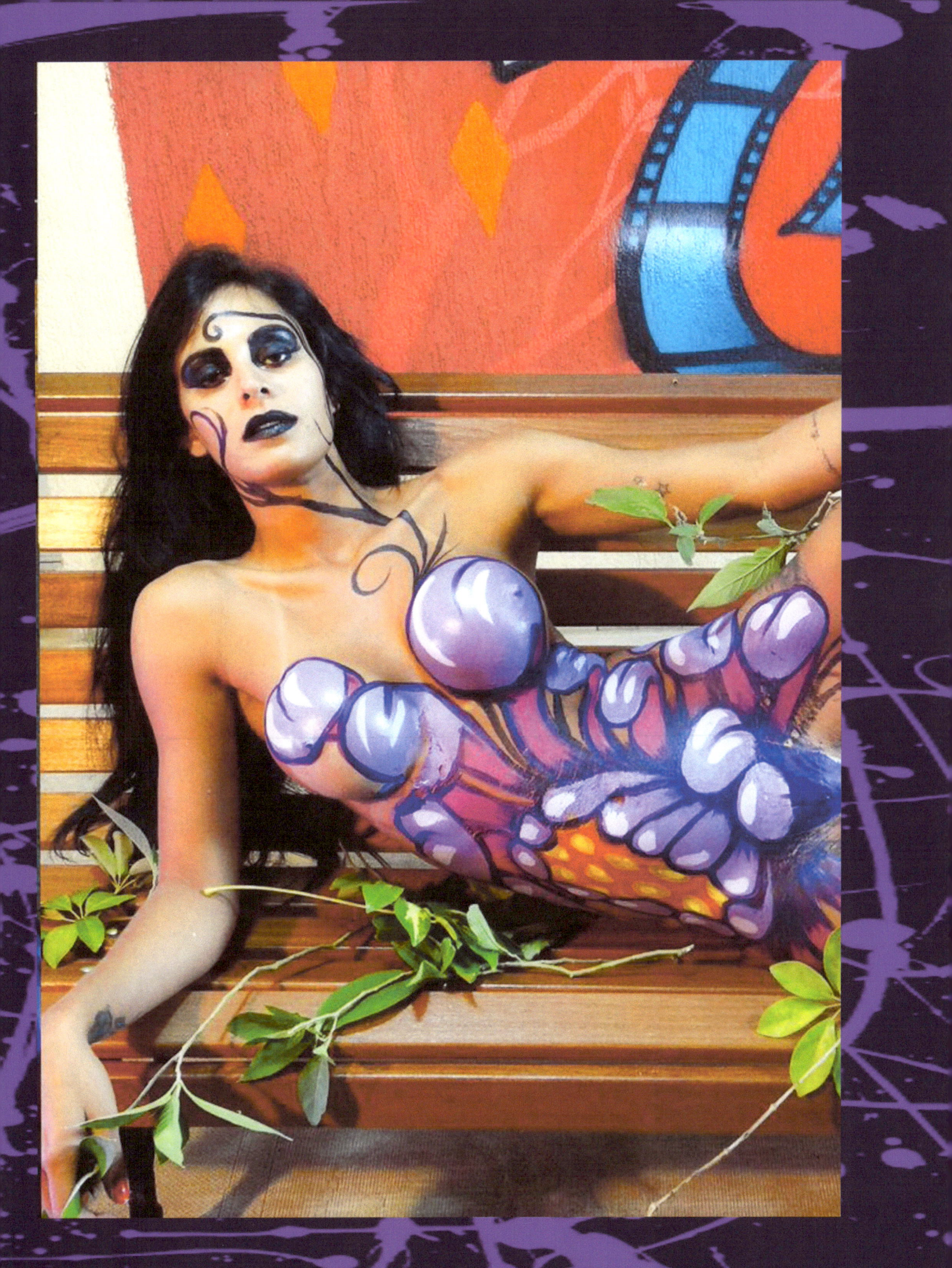

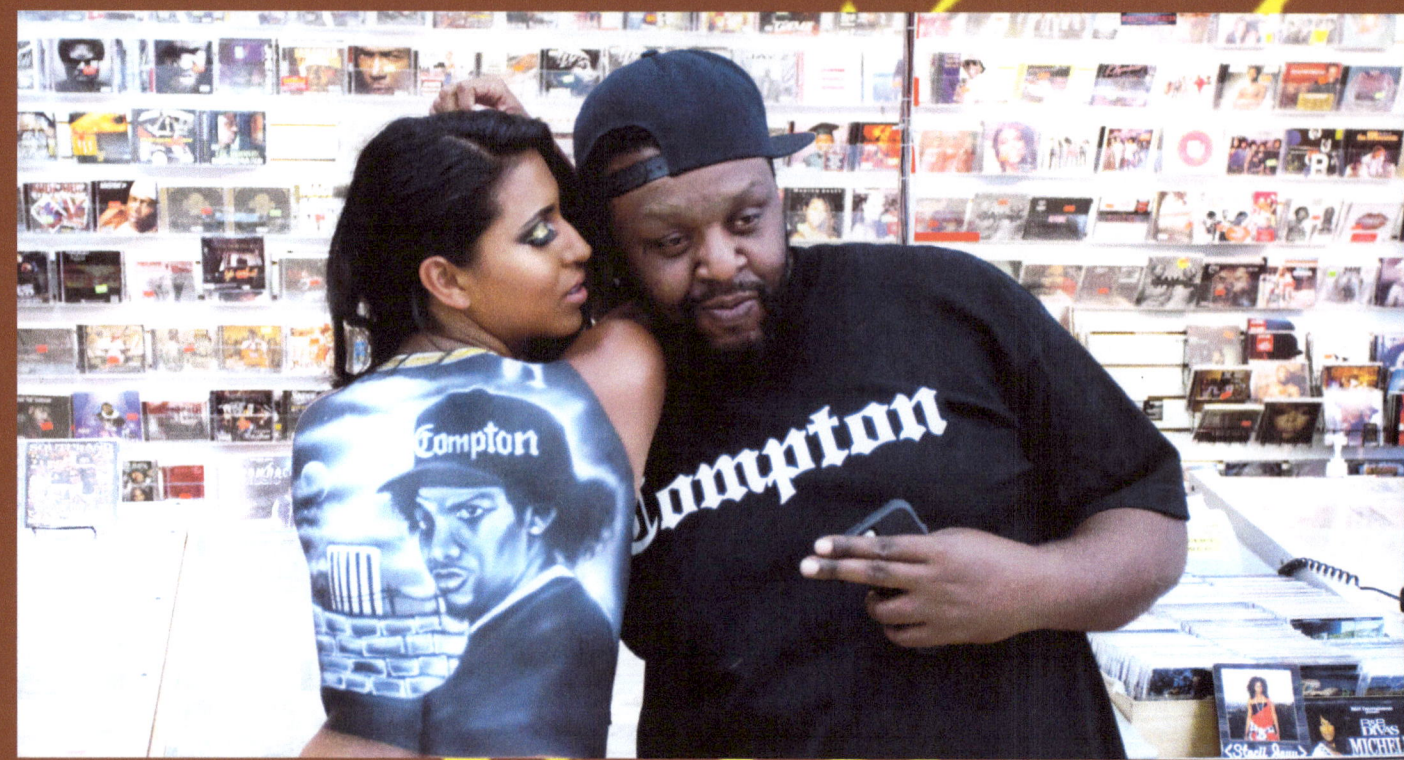

RISKIE
WWW.THAINKWELL.COM

A young man in Compton, California, like most young children, he began drawing and tracing images in coloring books. He had no idea at such a young age that the simple childhood pleasure, which he enjoyed, would be his claim to fame. Never abandoning his desire to be artistic, Riskie left the coloring books behind and became a graffiti writer; more commonly known as a tagger. It was Ms. Marta Farris, Riskie's high school art teacher, who encouraged Riskie to take his art more seriously. In time, she helped him study his craft to become more detailed so that his street approach to art could be viewed as fine art. Riskie decided to take his talents to the mall where he opened up a booth and began airbrushing designs for customers in the mall. The success rate was overwhelming and Riskie knew his dedication to his craft had finally paid off. His dedication caught the attention of Death Row CEO and rap mogul Suge Knight, who introduced him to Tupac Shakur. Riskie's first project for Death Row was the insert for the Tupac's *All Eyez On Me* album. Riskie was then commissioned to create the album cover for Tupac's newest release. Tupac shared with Riskie his vision for the album cover. Once Riskie had the idea sealed in his mind, he created one of the most talked-about album covers in the history of hip-hop for one of the illest and most influential albums in hip-hop. Tupac's *Makaveli: The 7 Day Theory*,

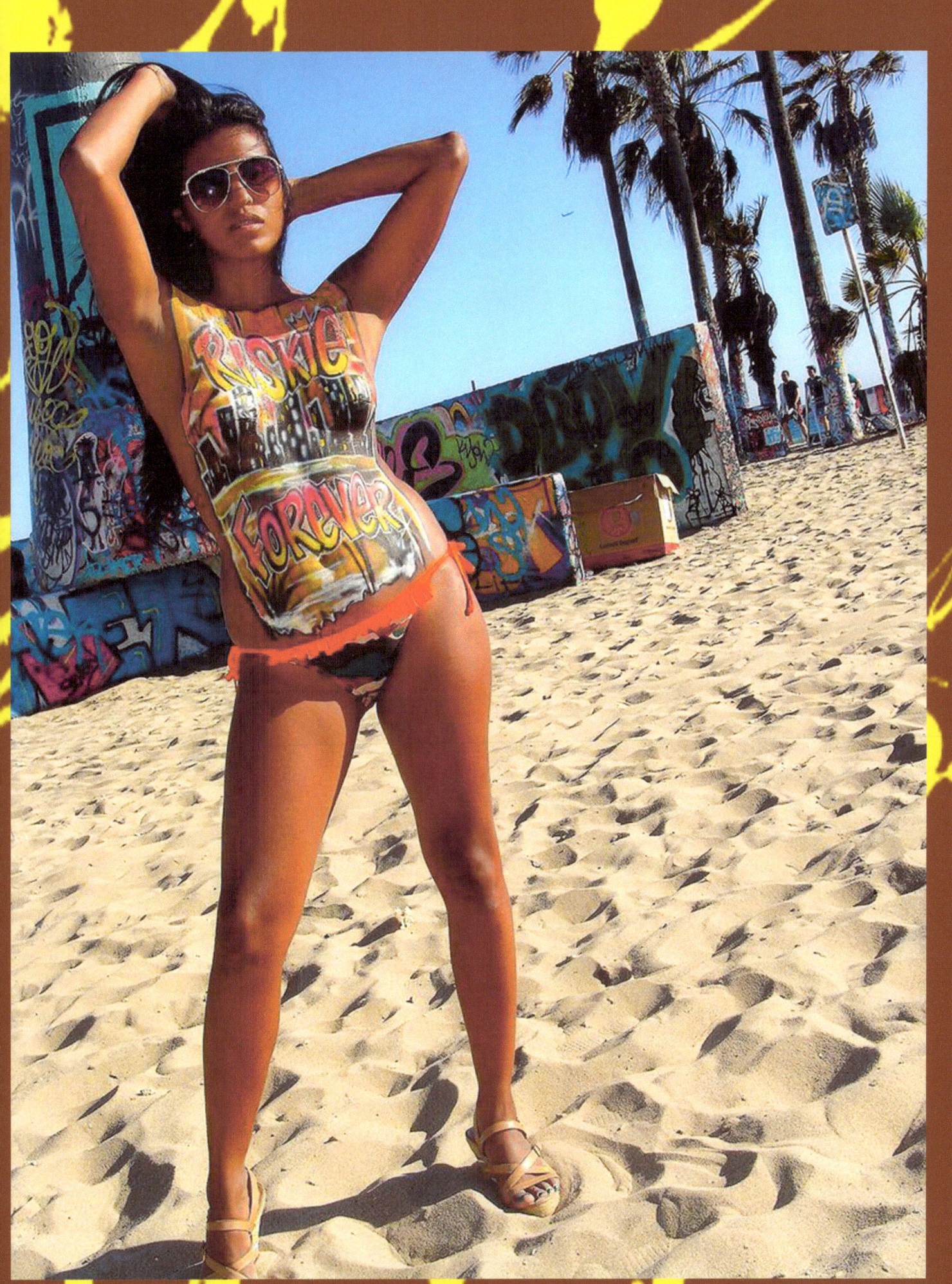

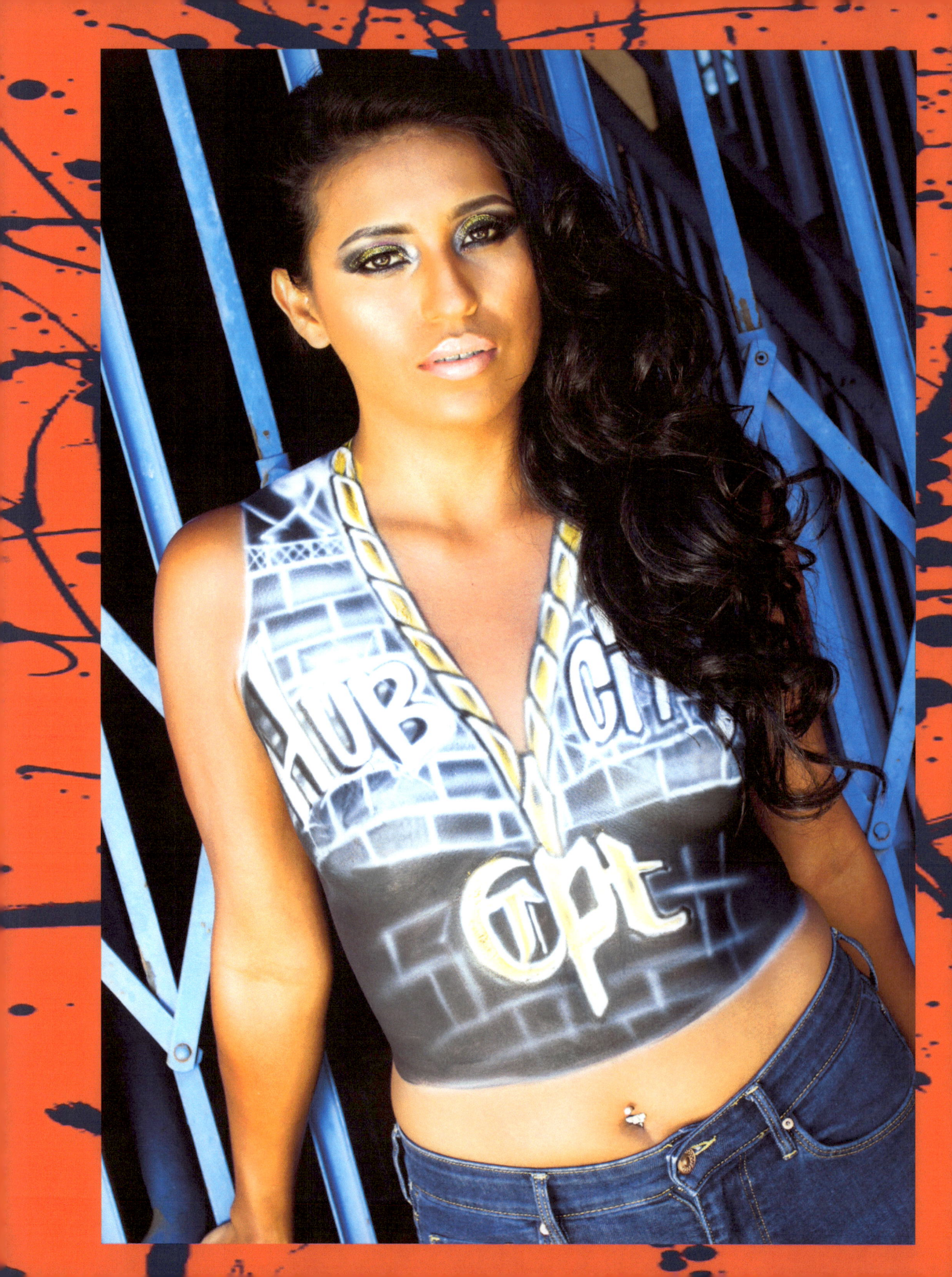

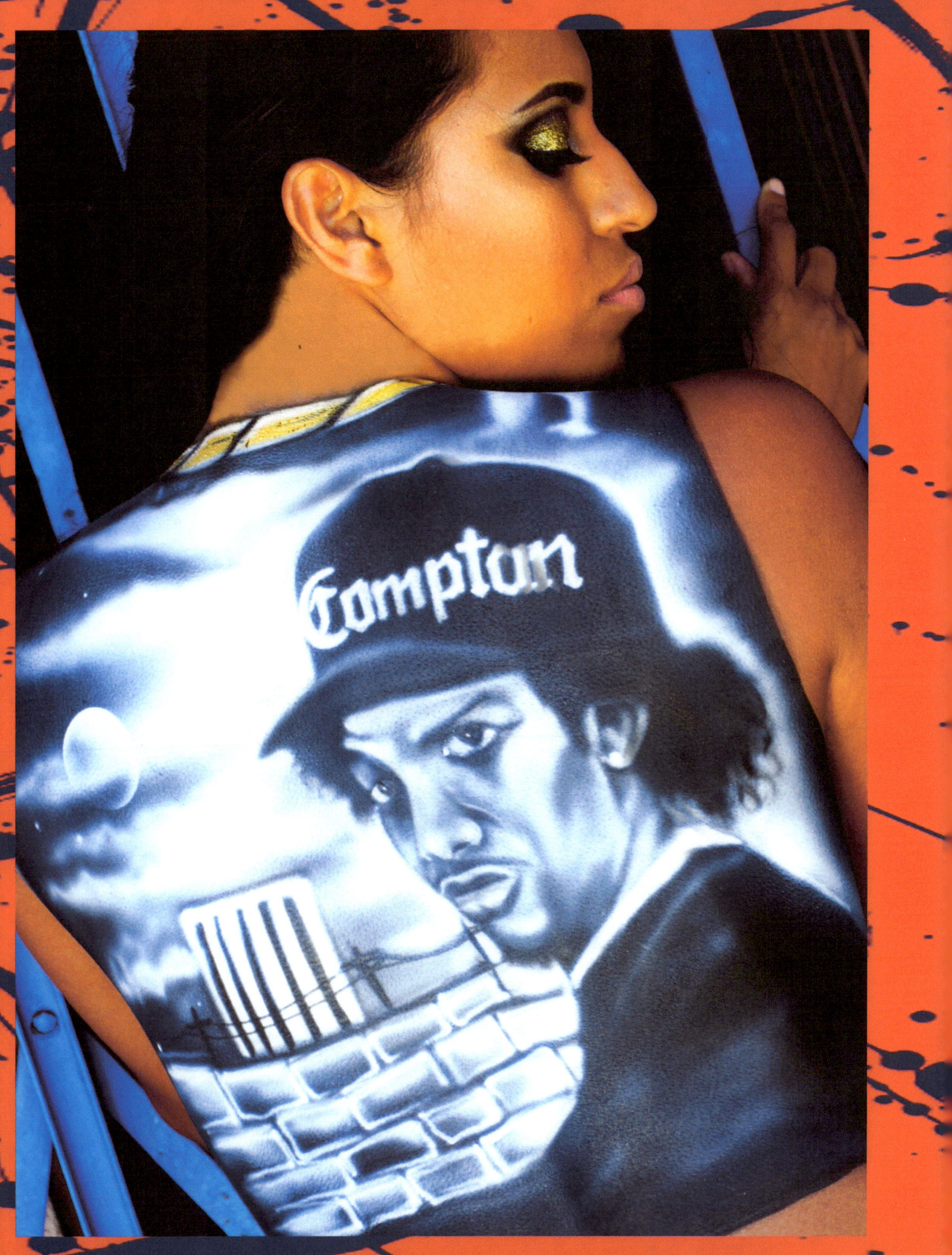

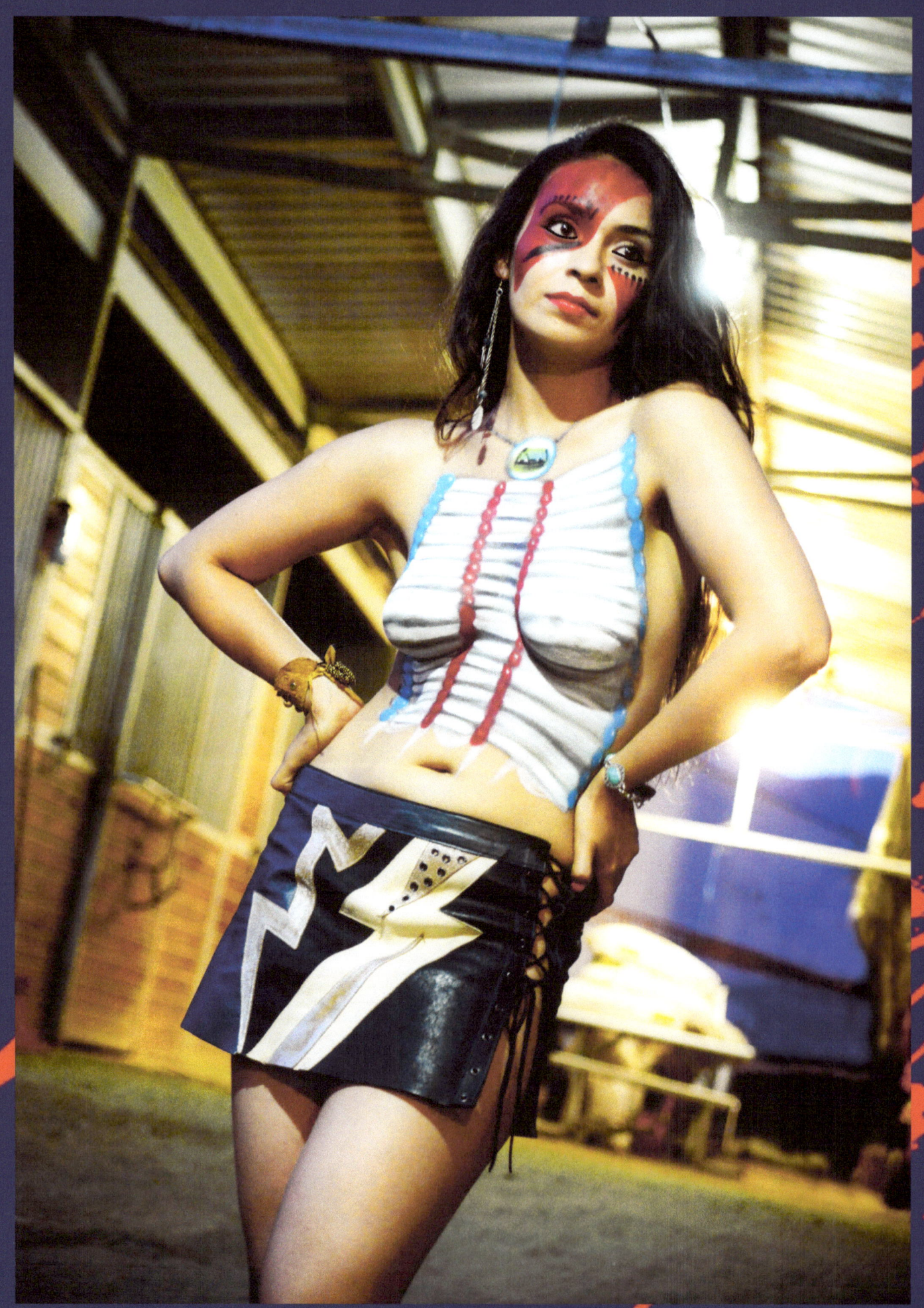

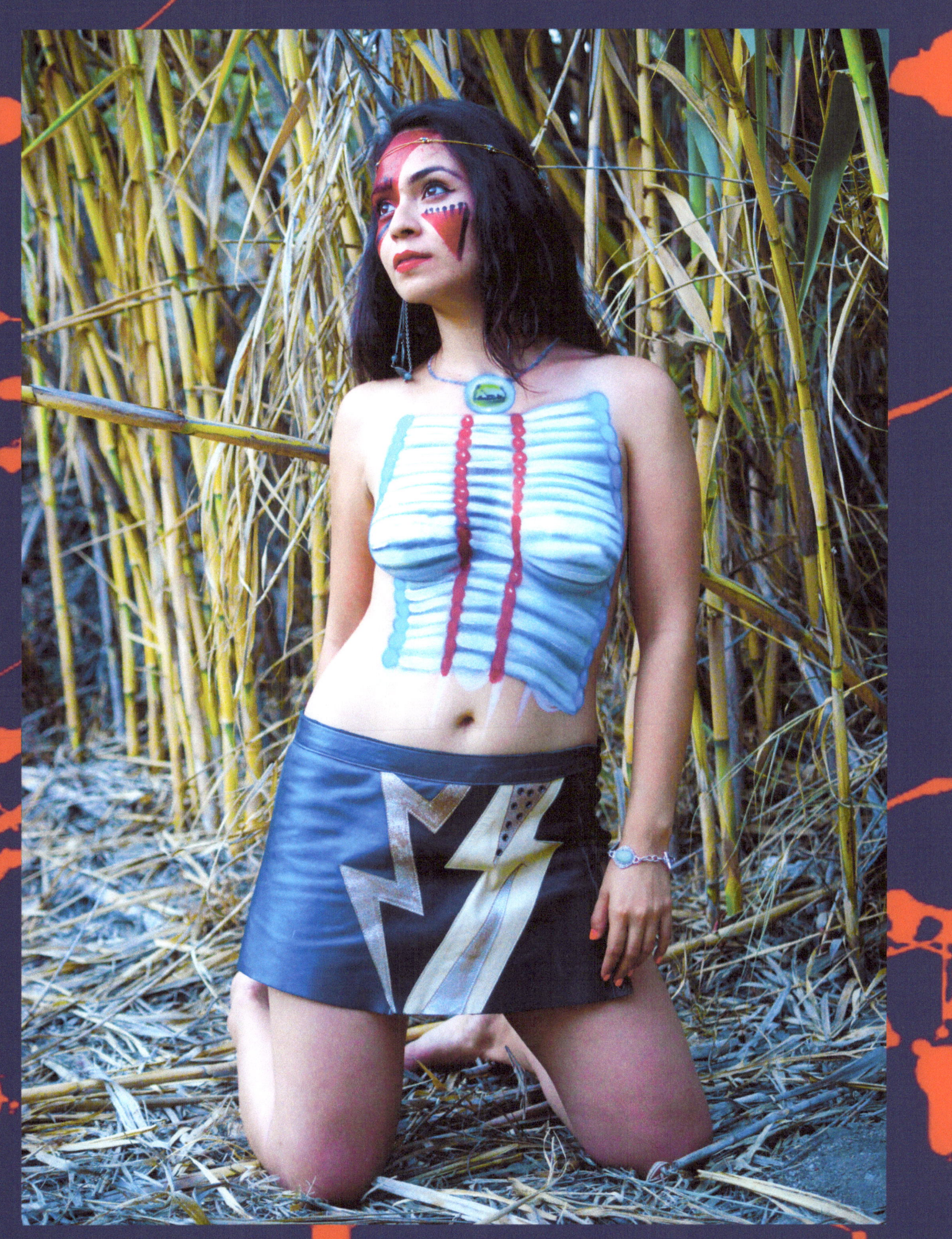

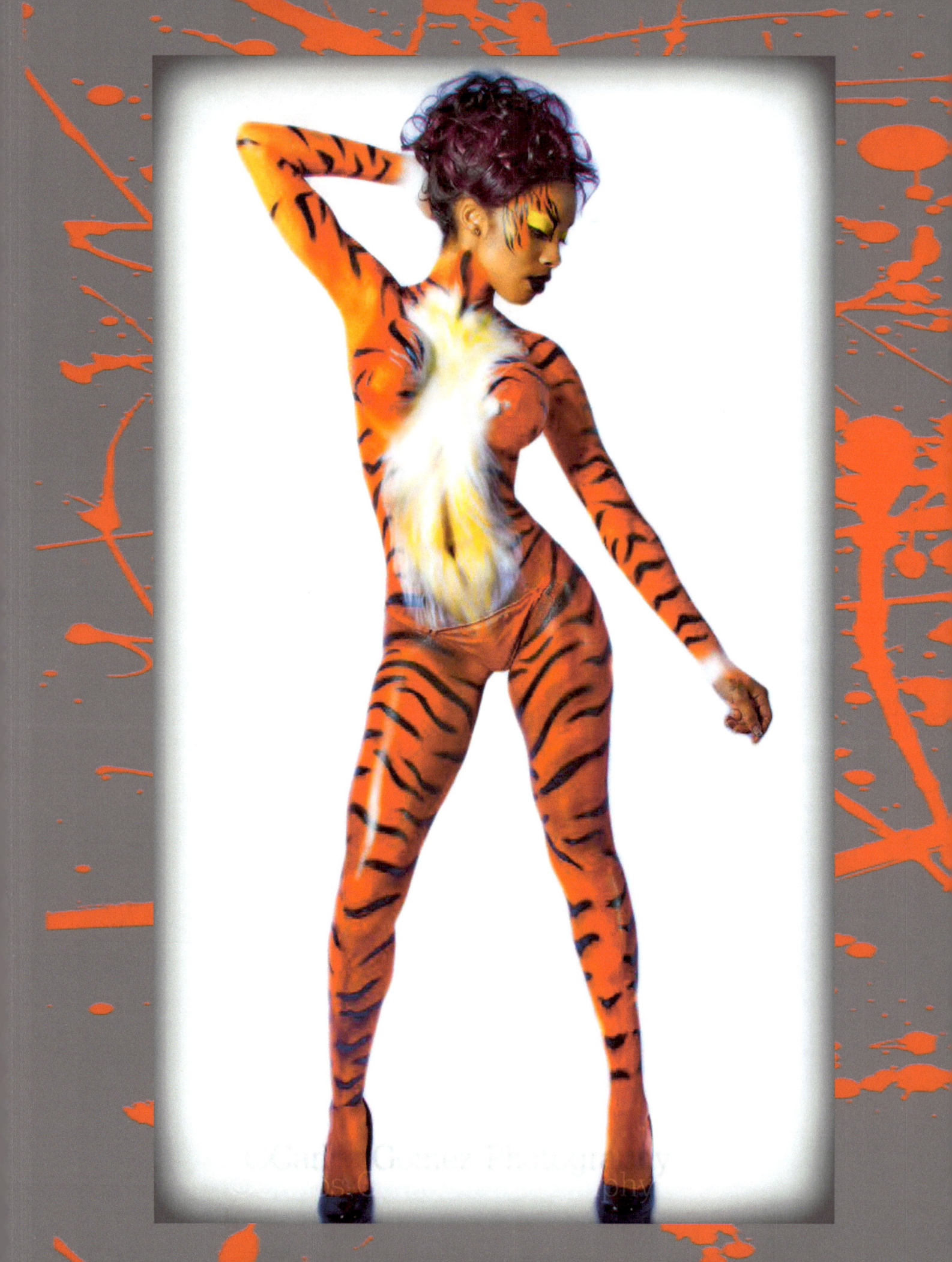

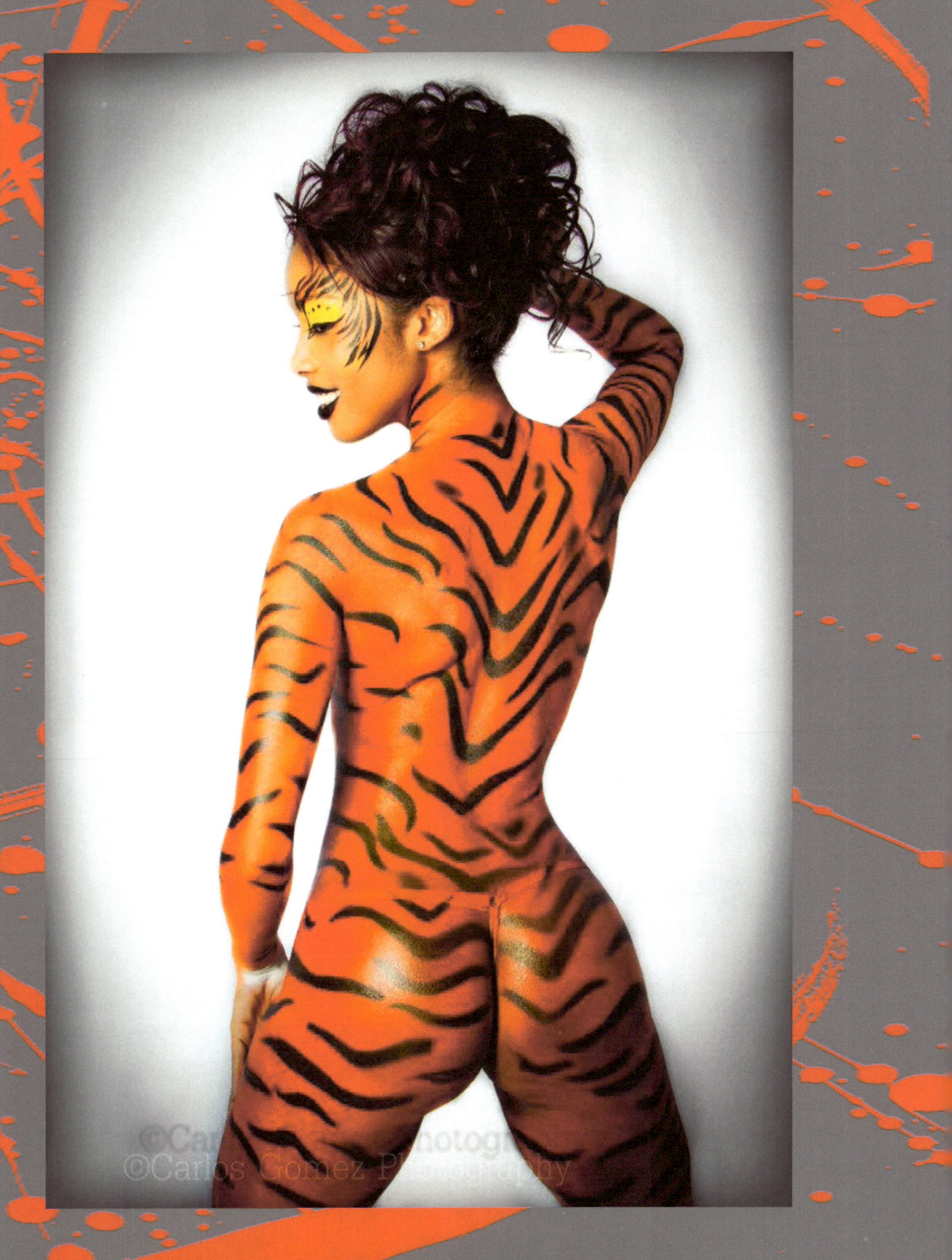

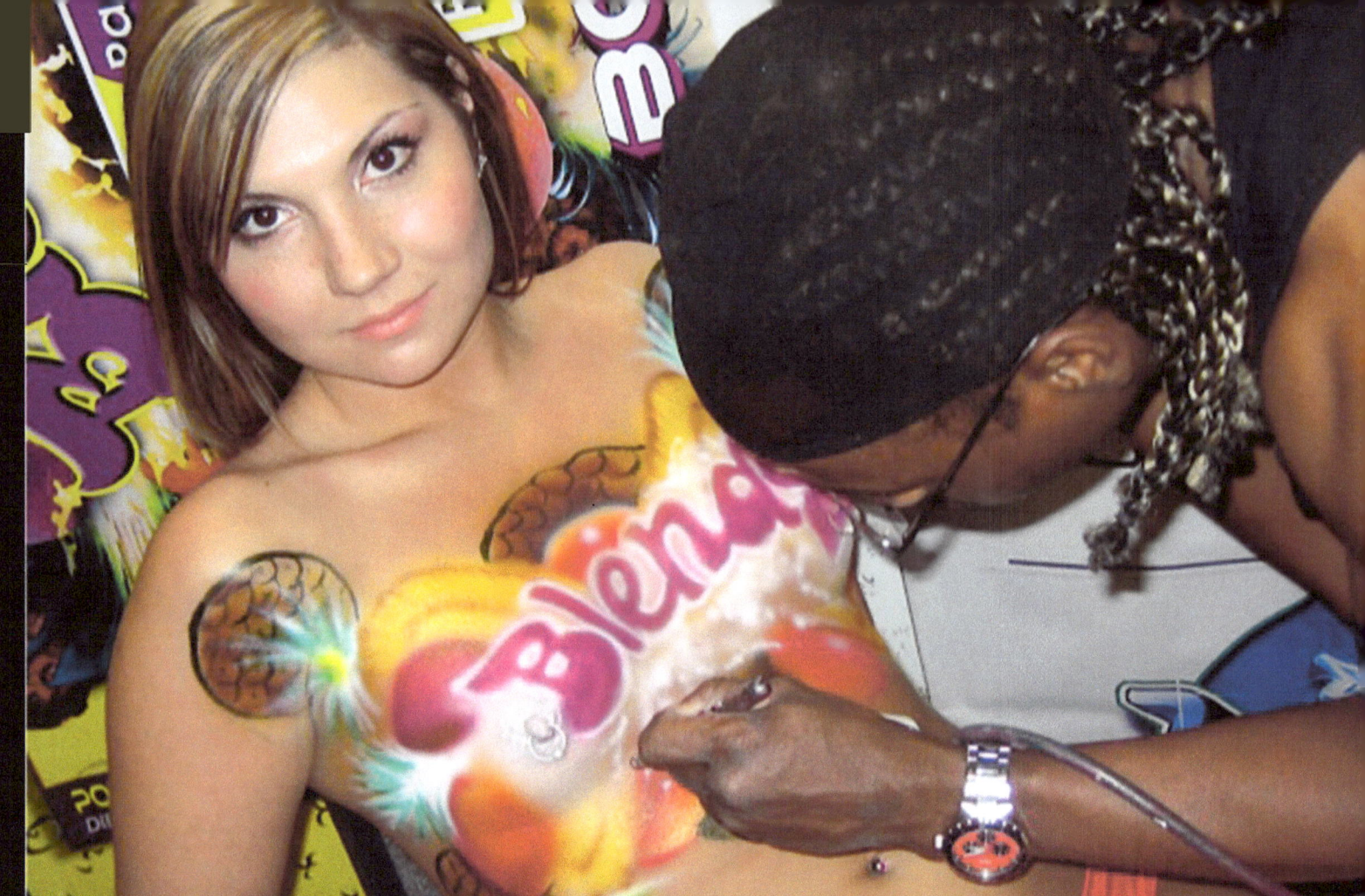

The Chaz Man
WWW.THECHAZMAN.COM

First and foremost, I am not just a body paint artist. I'm an artist. I paint on canvas. I paint on clothes. I paint murals. I'm a photographer. And I'm also a musician. This body painting journey was simply a mistake!!! It was never a part of my plan back in high school when I made a declaration to myself that I was going to be an artist and musician until the day I die. Body painting for

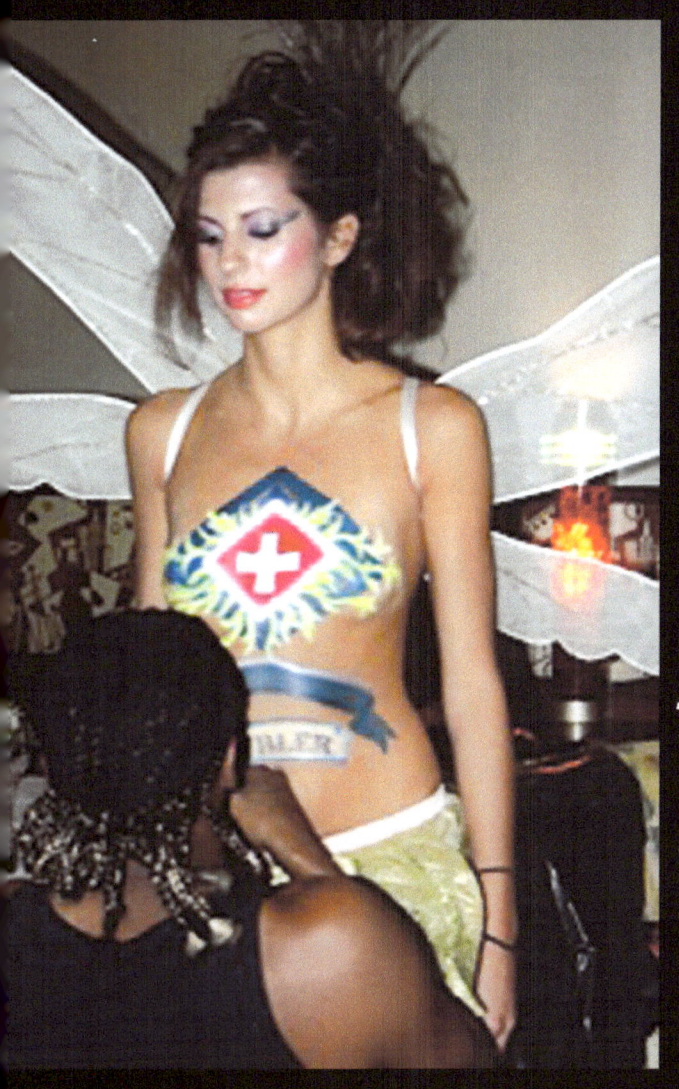 me simply came from Hugh Hefner and the Playboy mansion. I was watching E! television one day and they did a story on Hefner and the Playboy mansion and for the first time, I saw girls who were body painted at his amazing parties. Since I'm already an artist, I figure I would give it a go. I would find girls off craigslist and I would paint them, just for fun. From that, I decided to put pictures up online and make a small website. The next thing I know, I get a call from comedian Steve Harvey and his radio show to do a party here in Hollywood.

I was simply blown away. I made $3000 on that first body paint gig and took that money and started my own business. From that, Maxim magazine called me out of the blue. They loved my work so much they had me do many of their parties all over Los Angeles, San Diego, and in Puerto Rico. I took pictures of all the models and then put them on the website. Now the phone kept ringing from all parts of the country. I was being hired to body paint for American Express, Macy's, Marshalls, Absolut vodka, the GRAMMYs®, the Latin GRAMMYs®, and even Khloe Kardashian. I have body painted for many conventions, such as Comic-Con and E3. I have been on Spanish TV channels Telemundo and Univision. I've been hired by Fox to body paint at several Super Bowl parties.

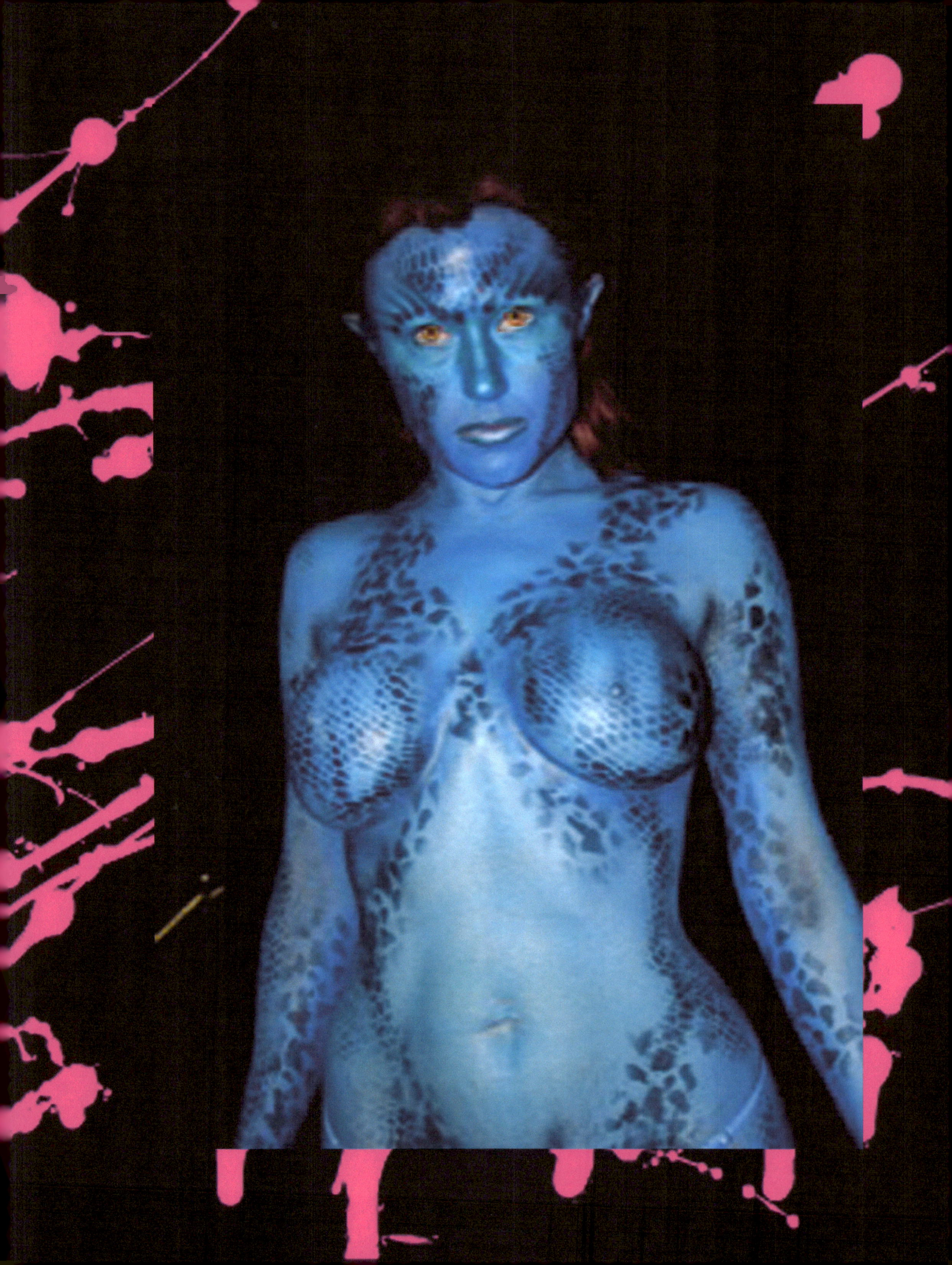

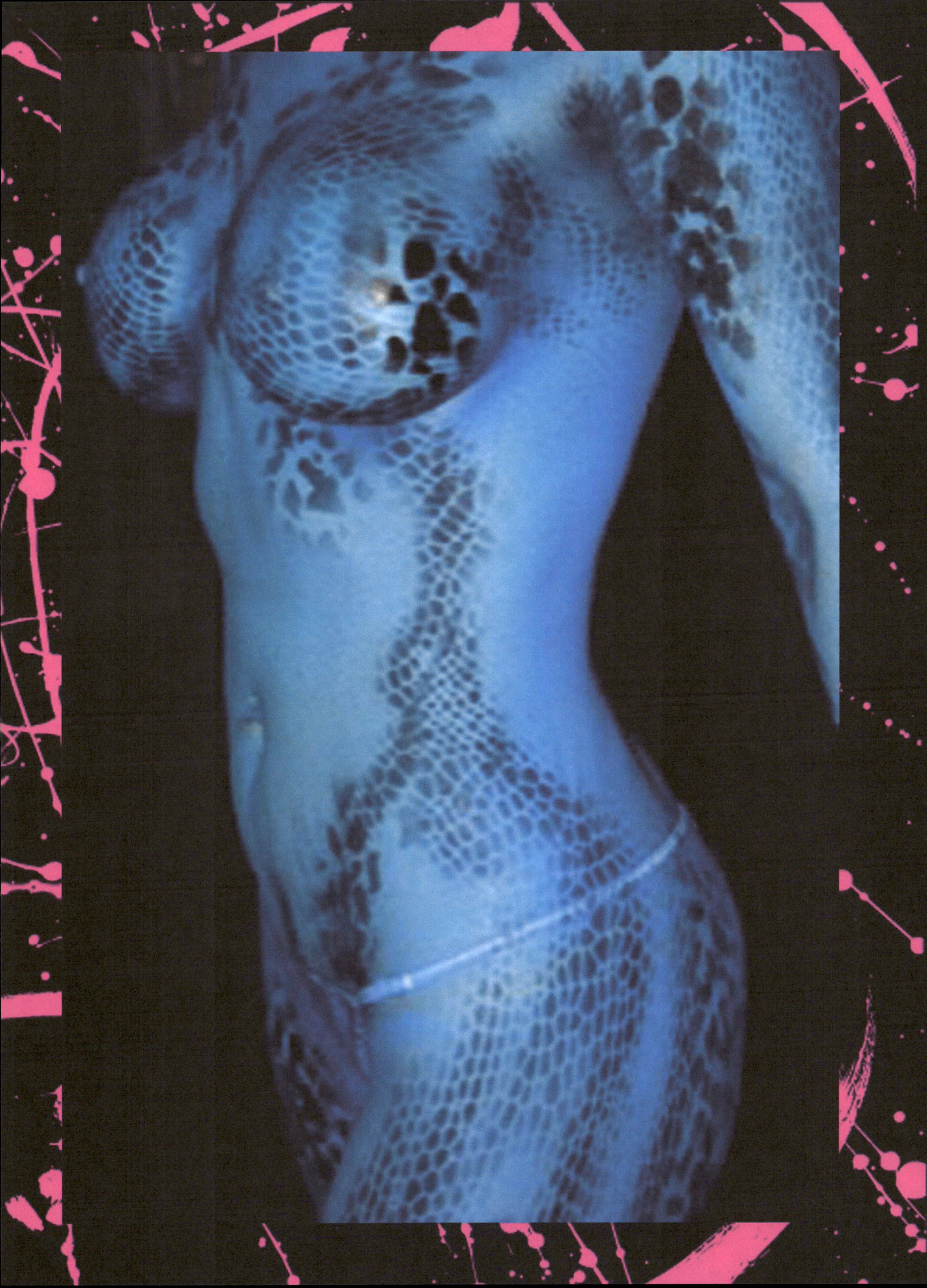

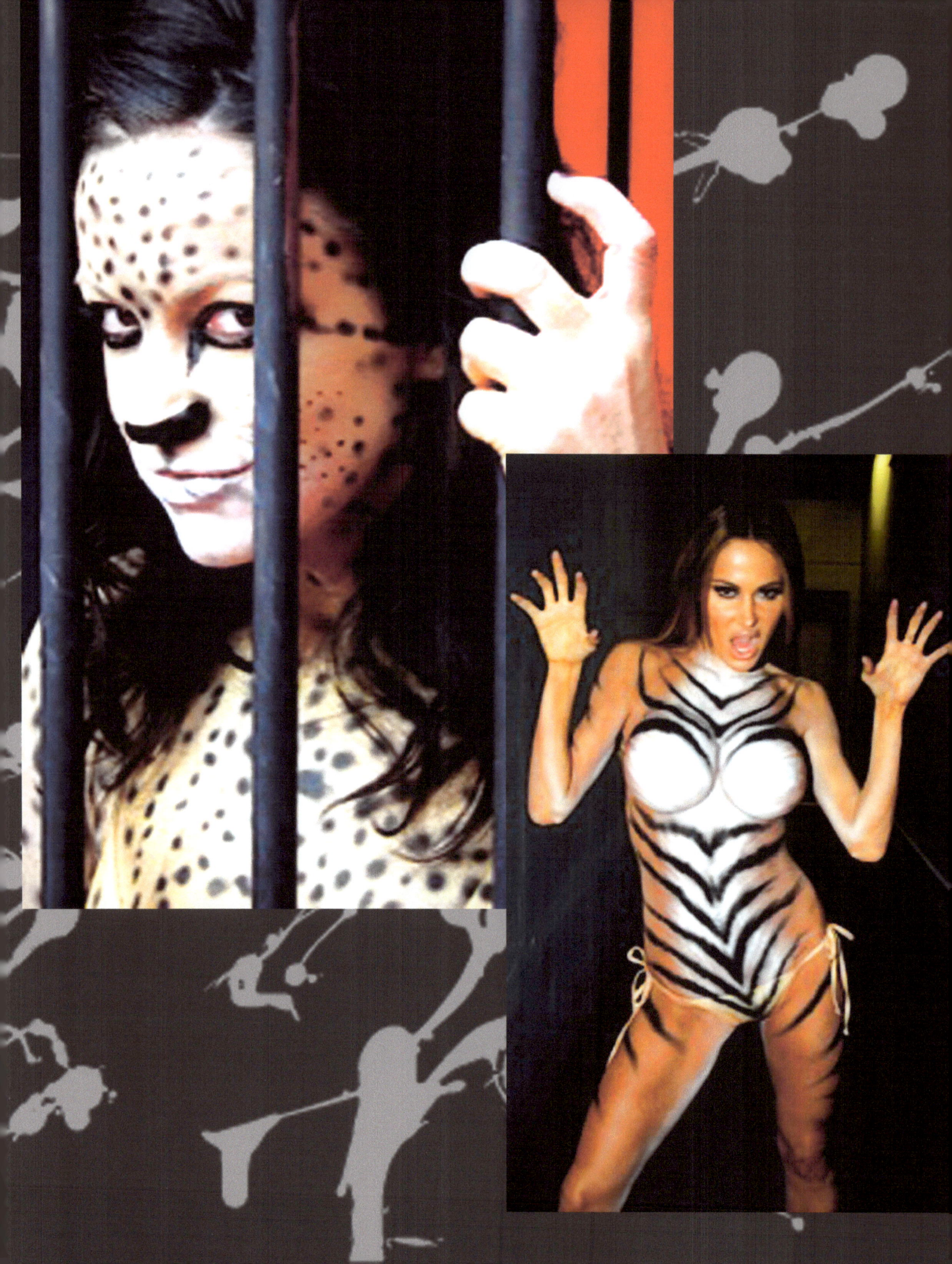

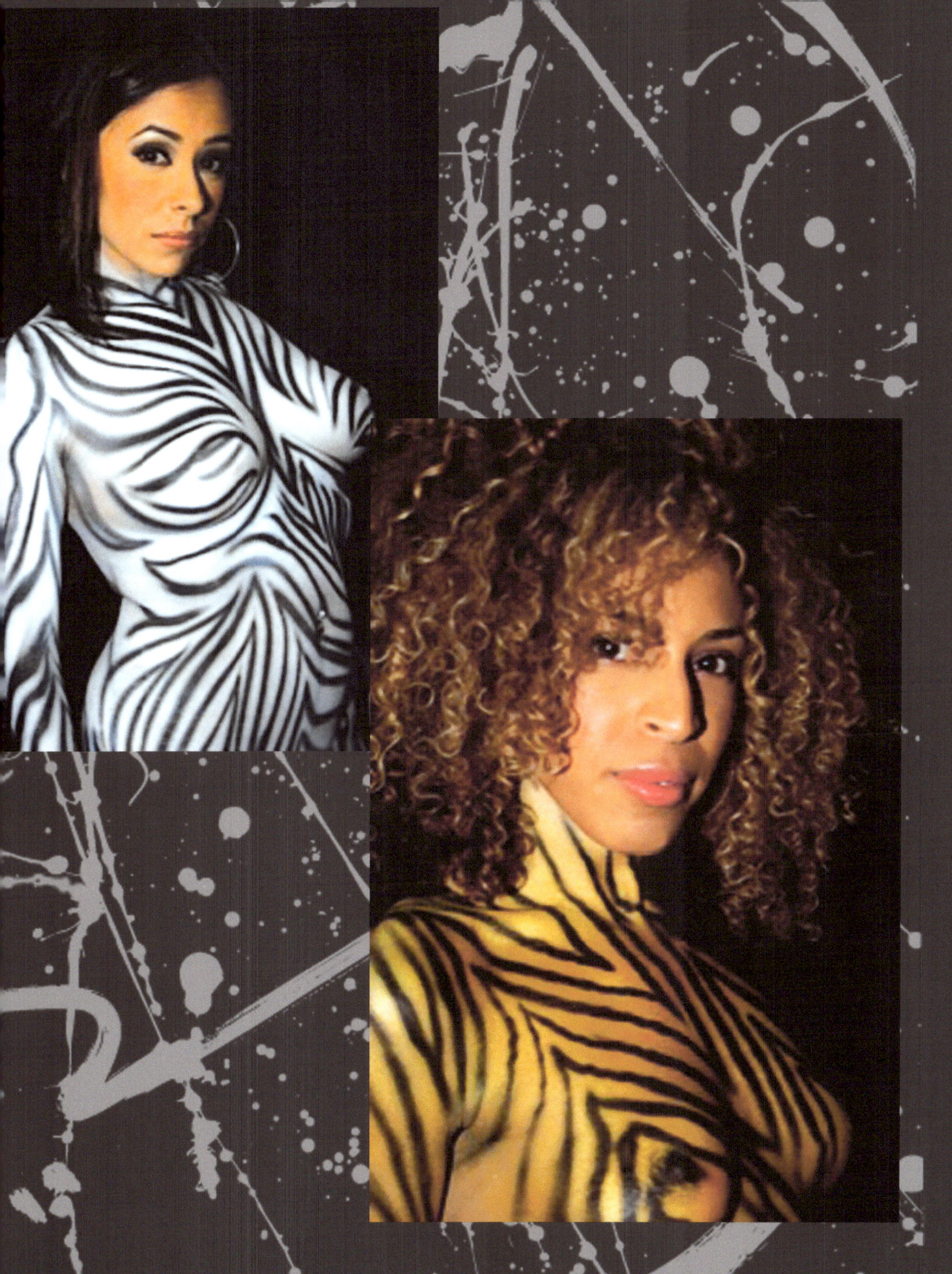

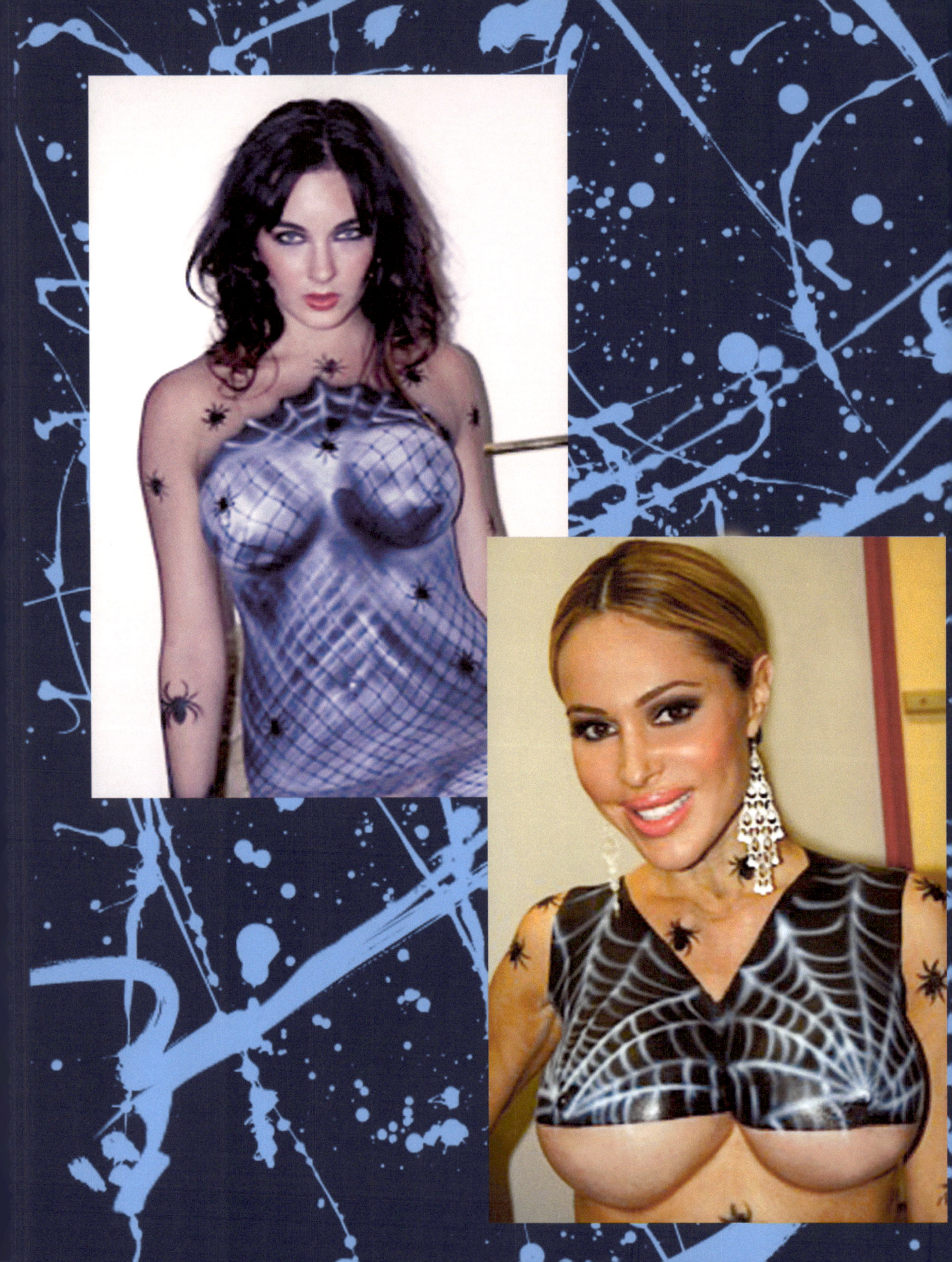

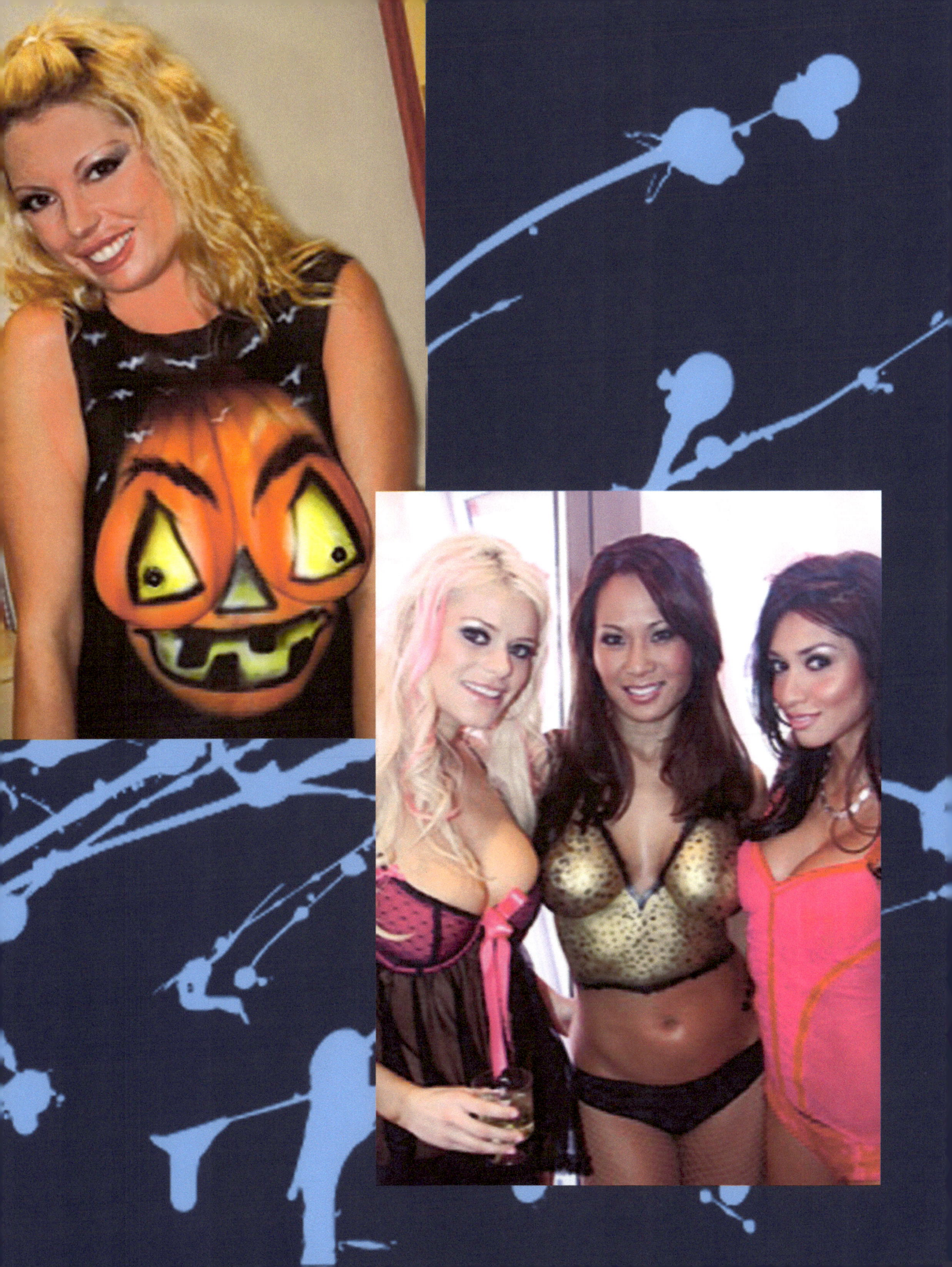

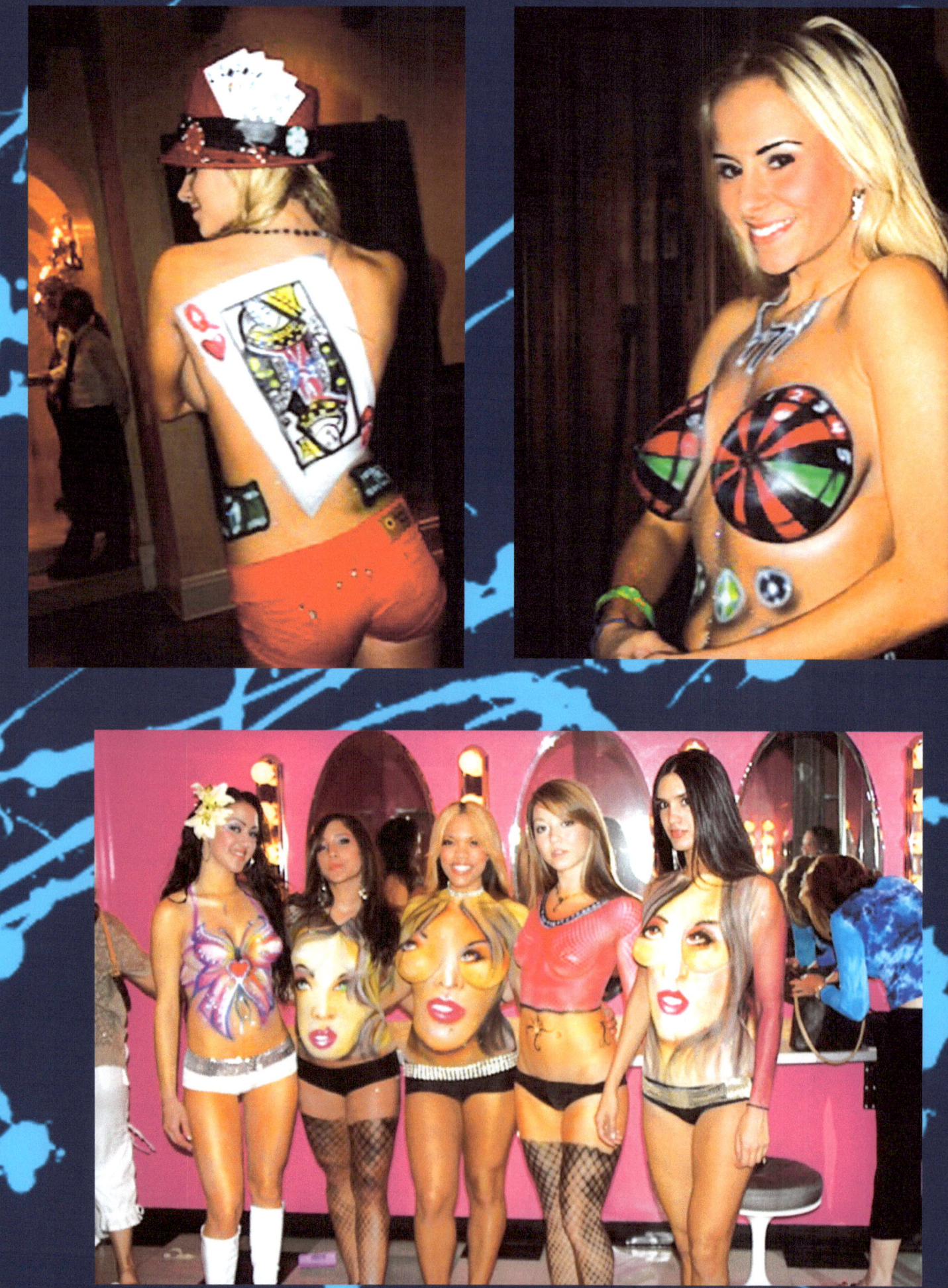

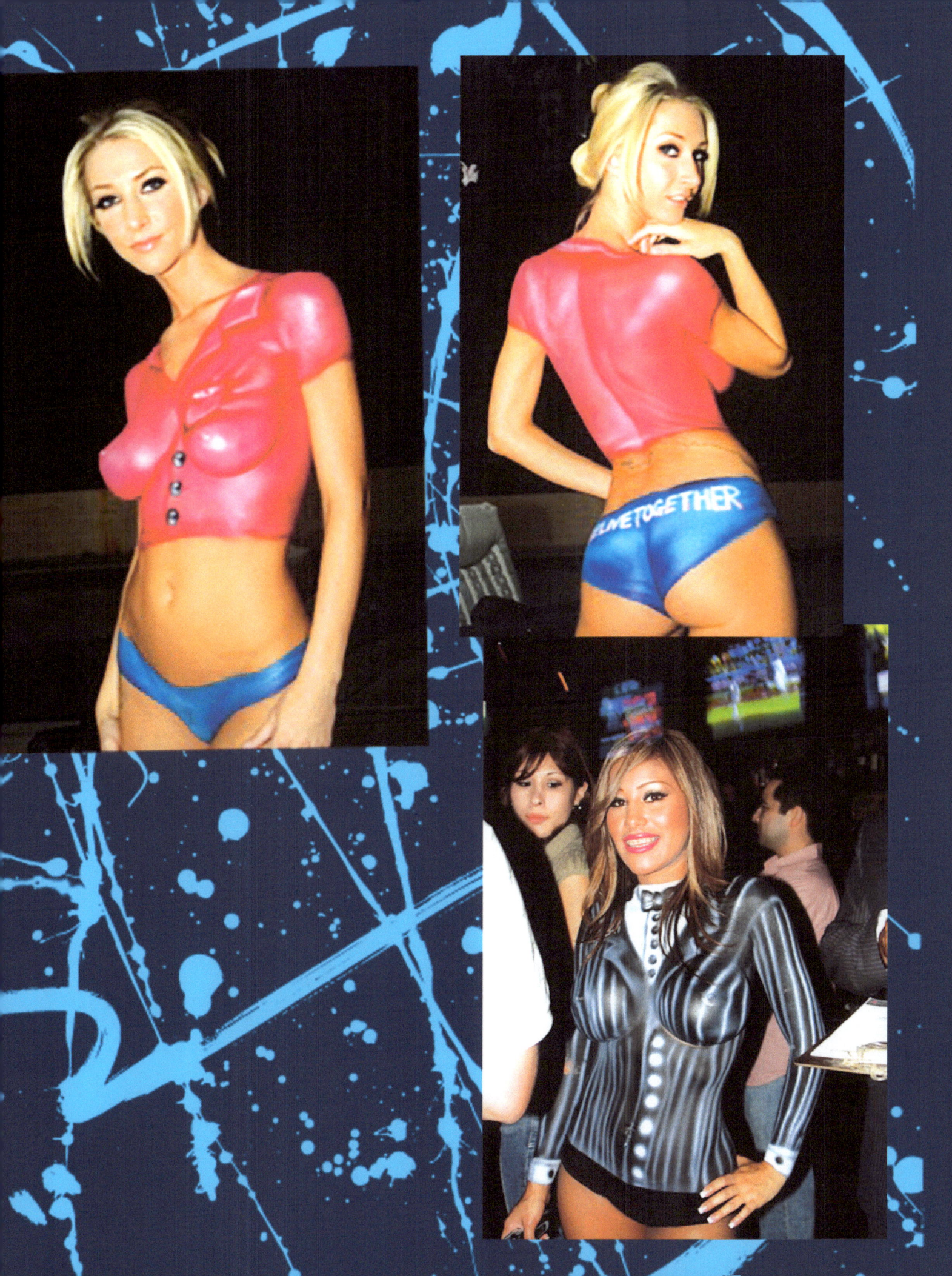

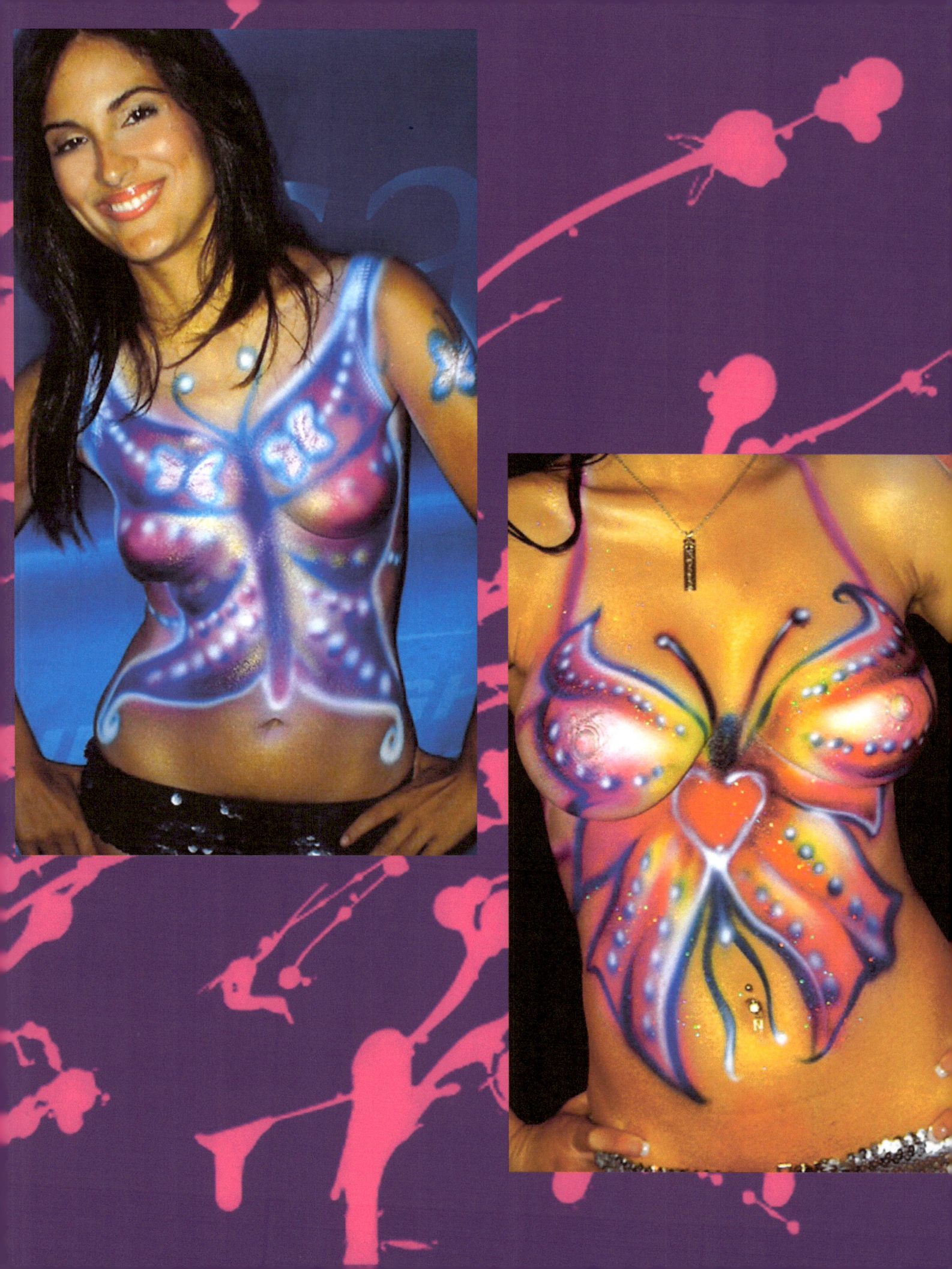

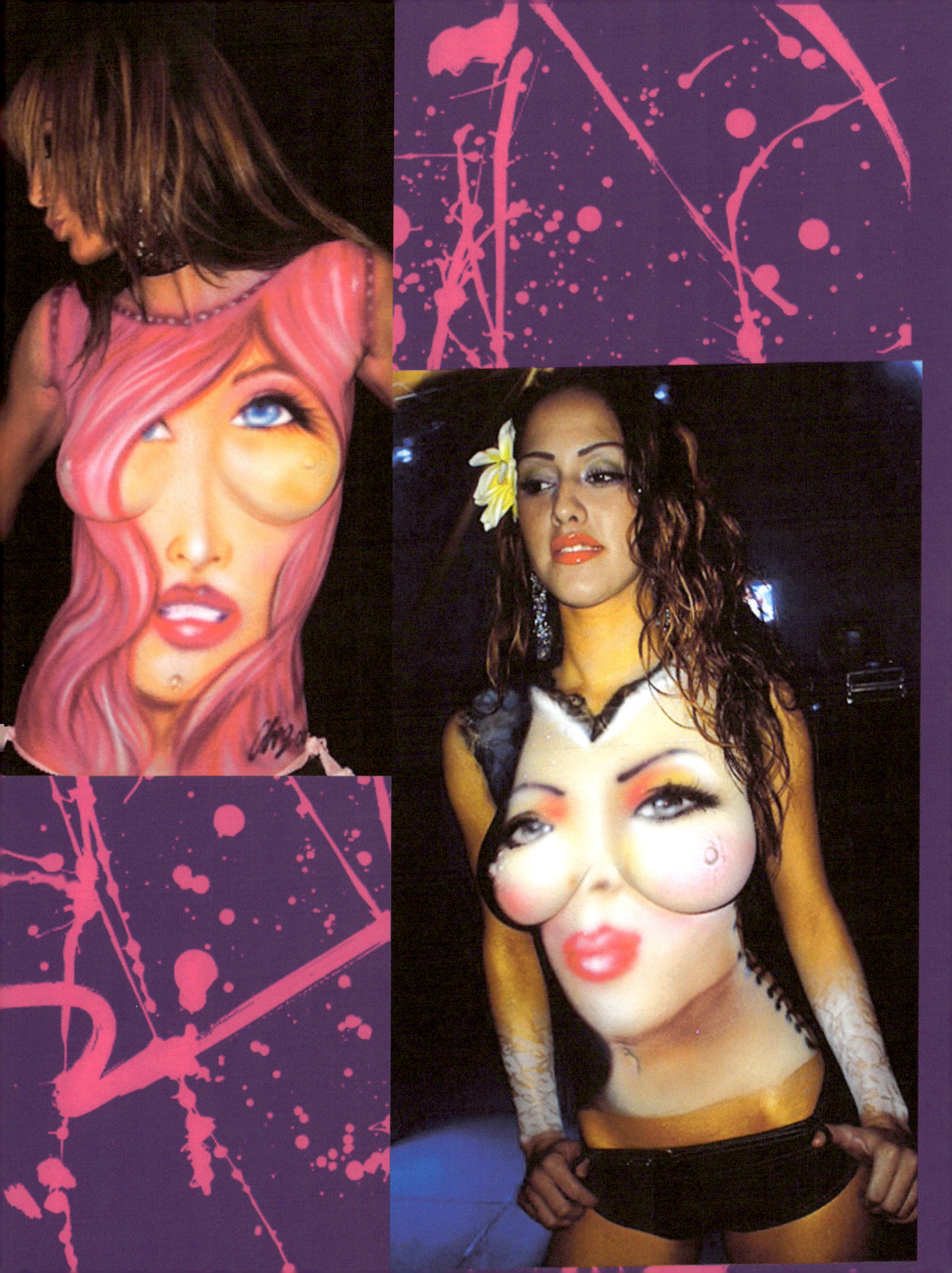

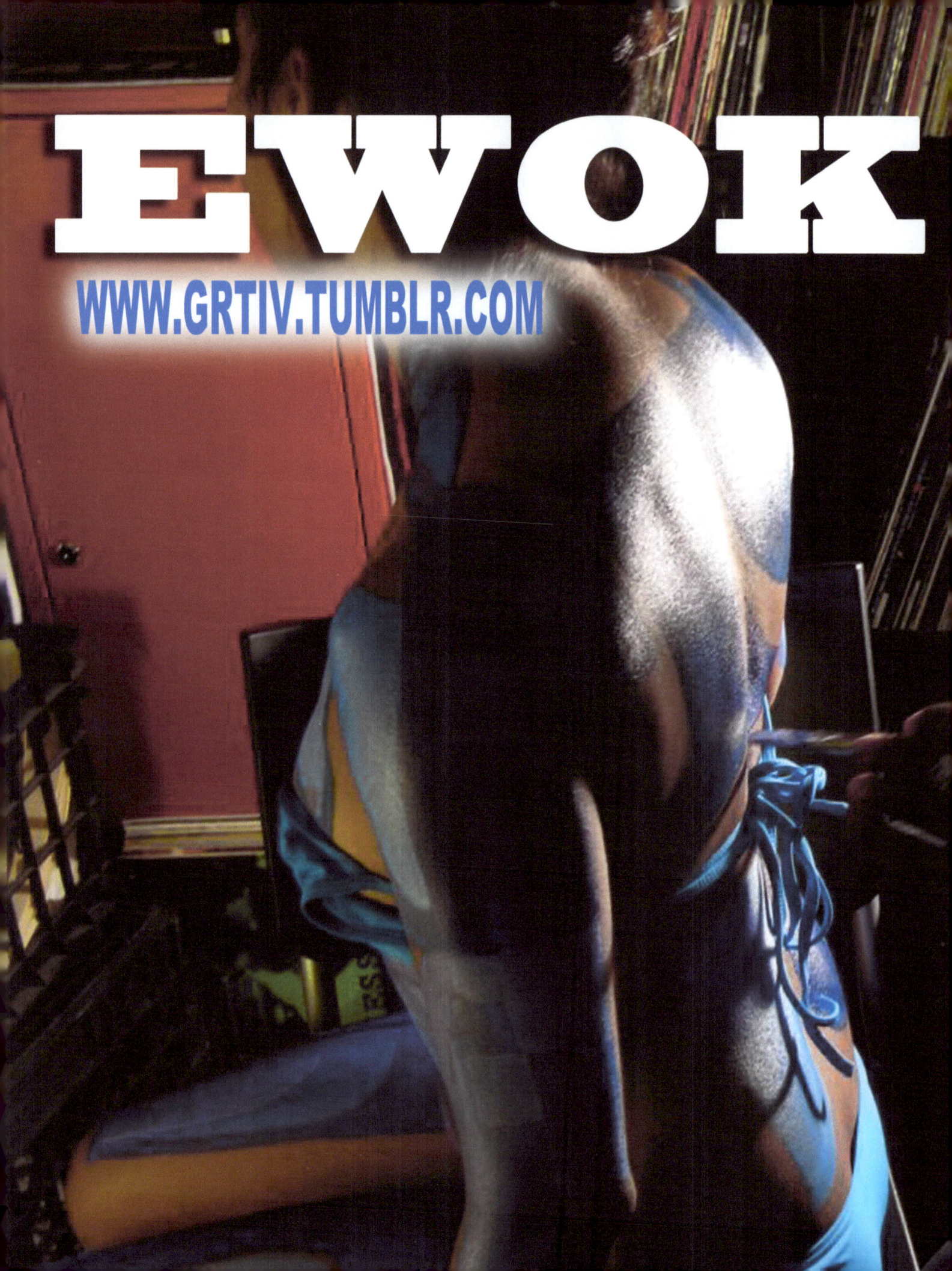

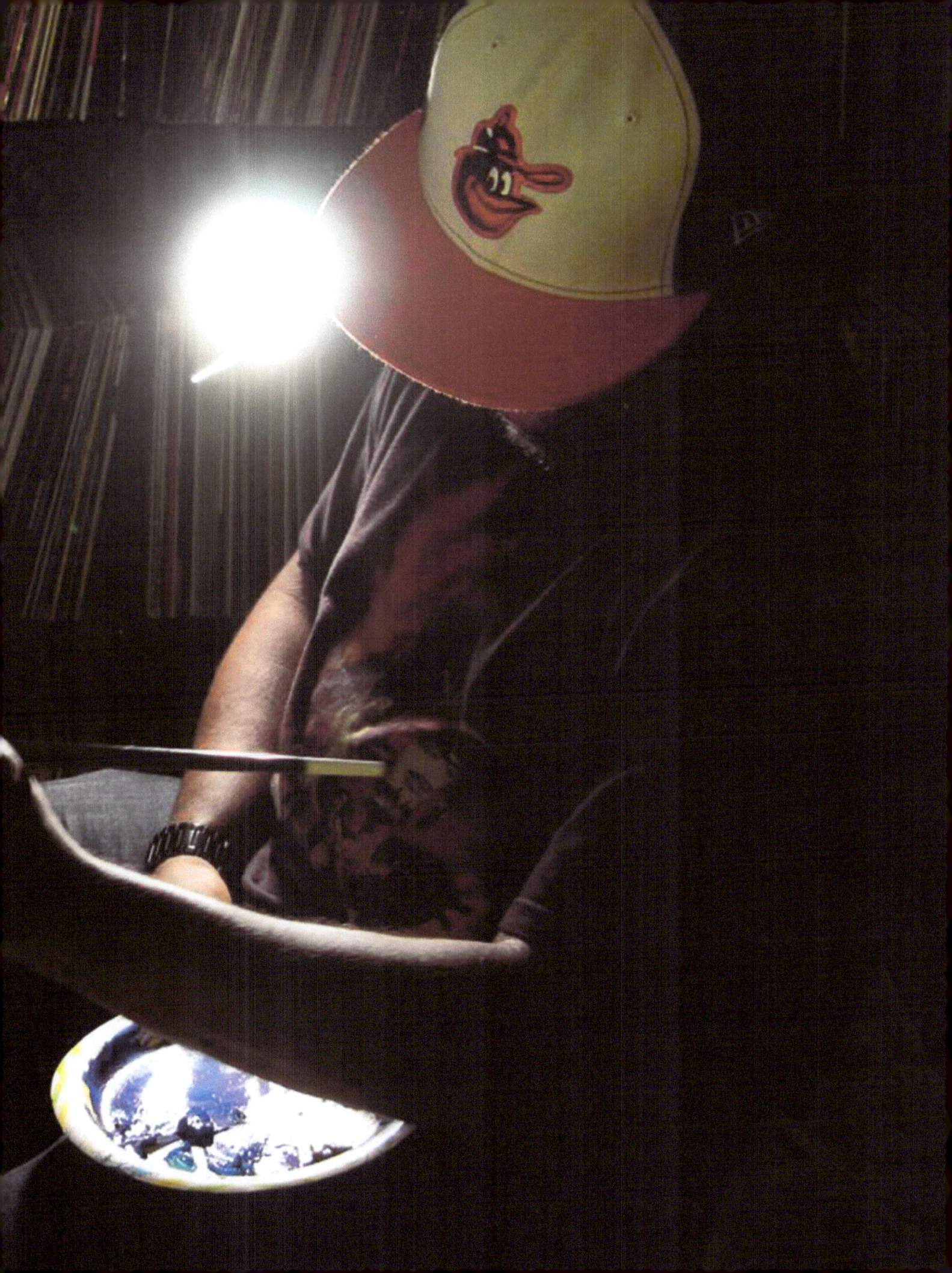

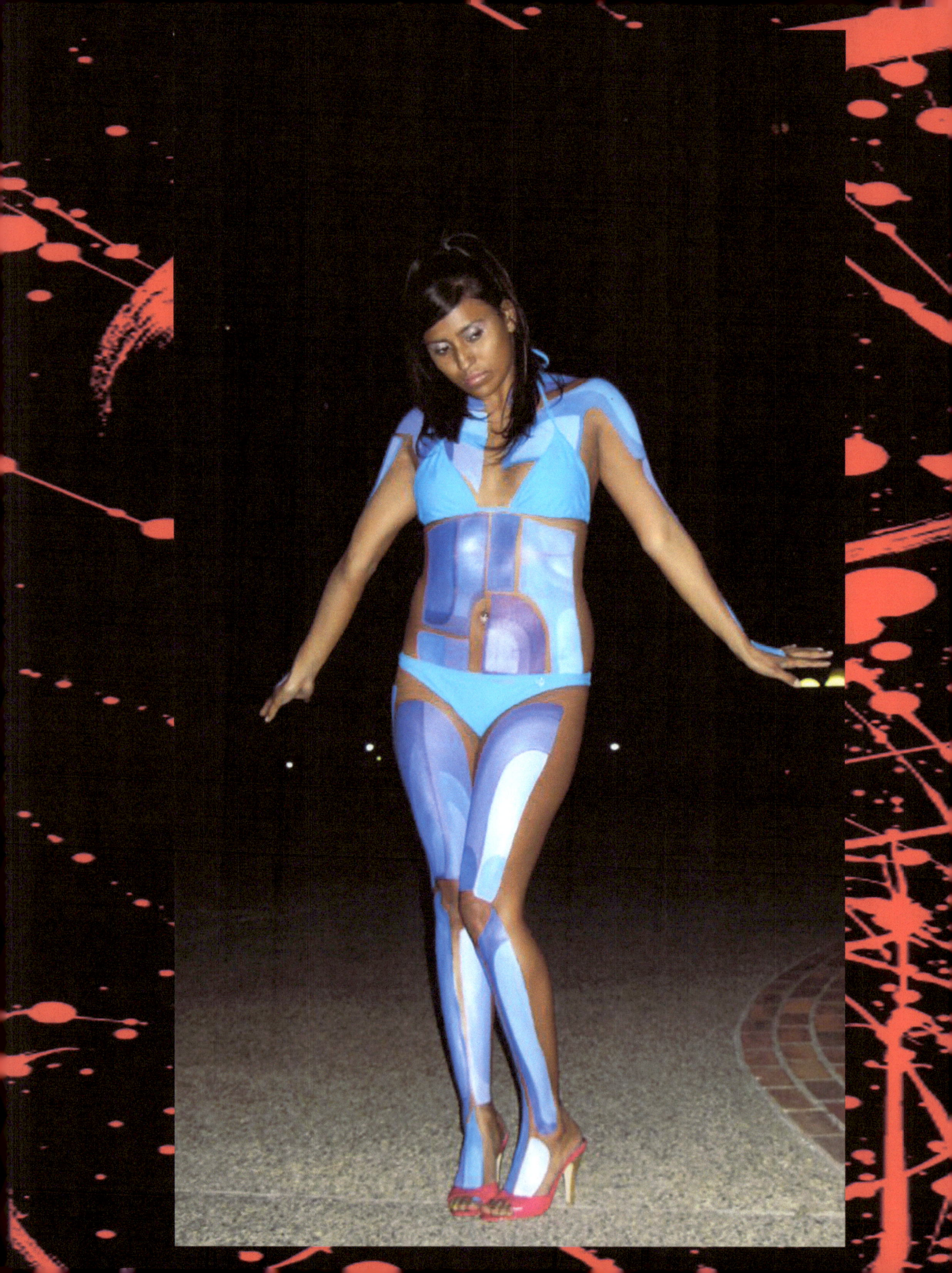

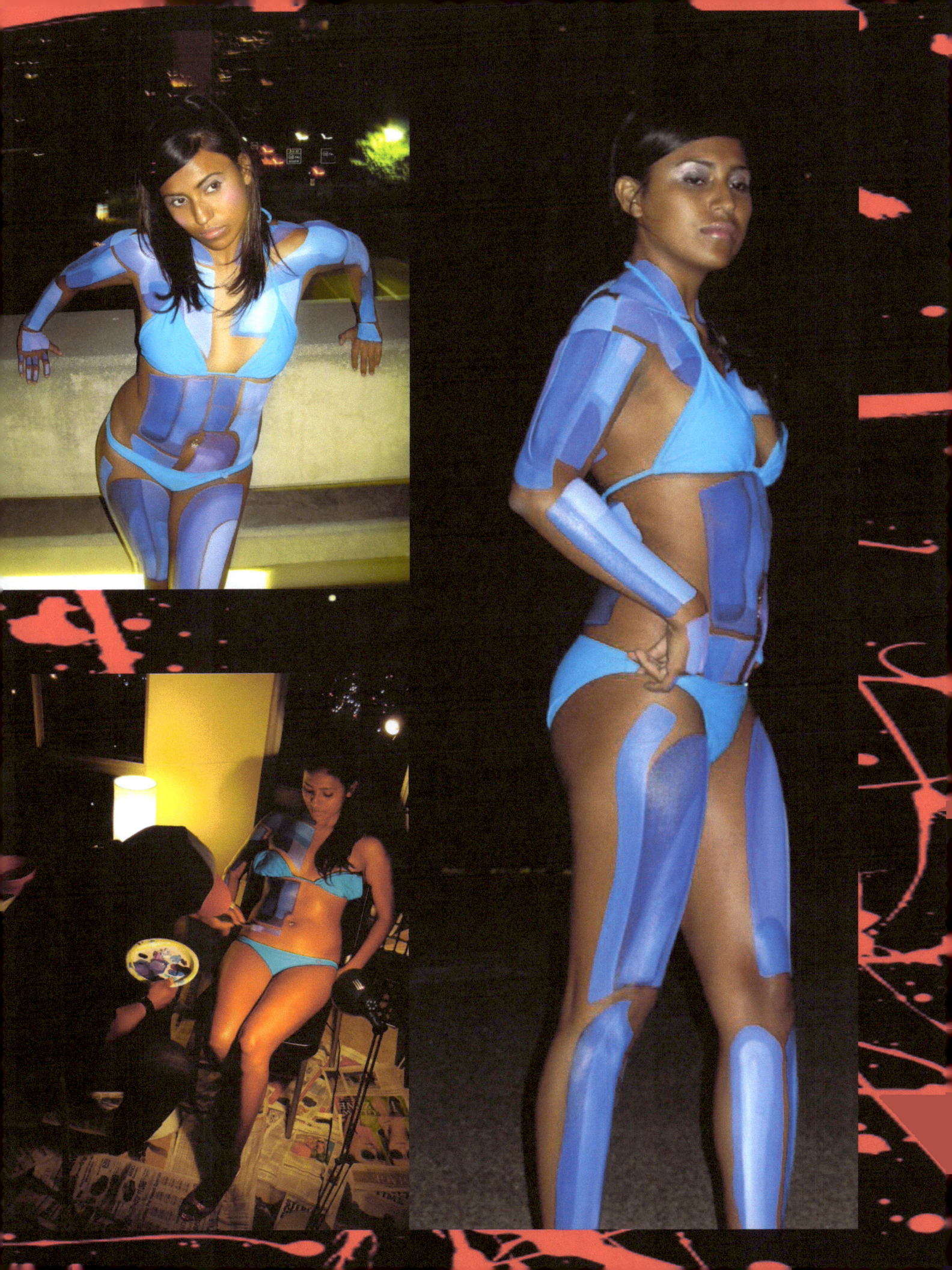

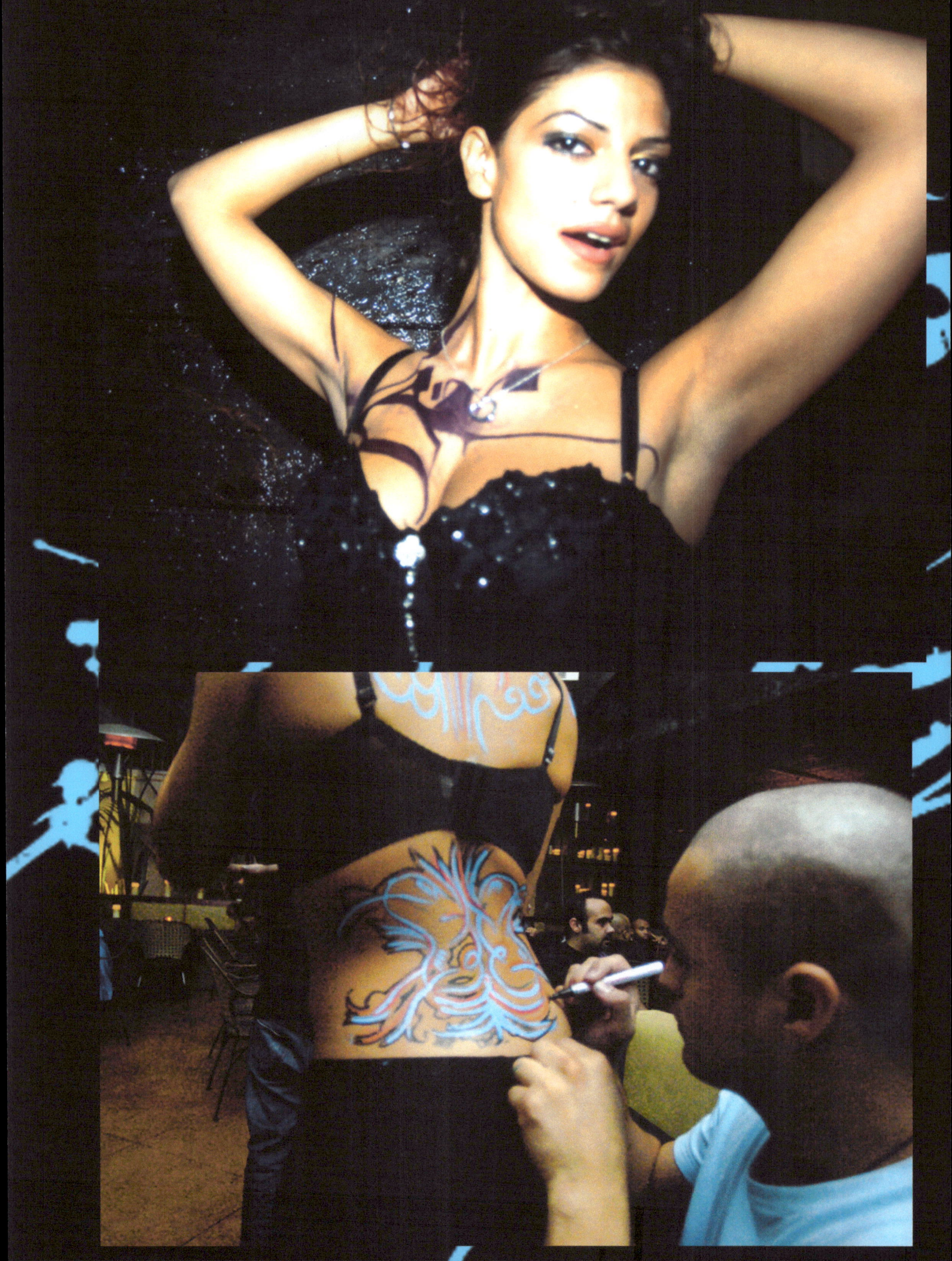

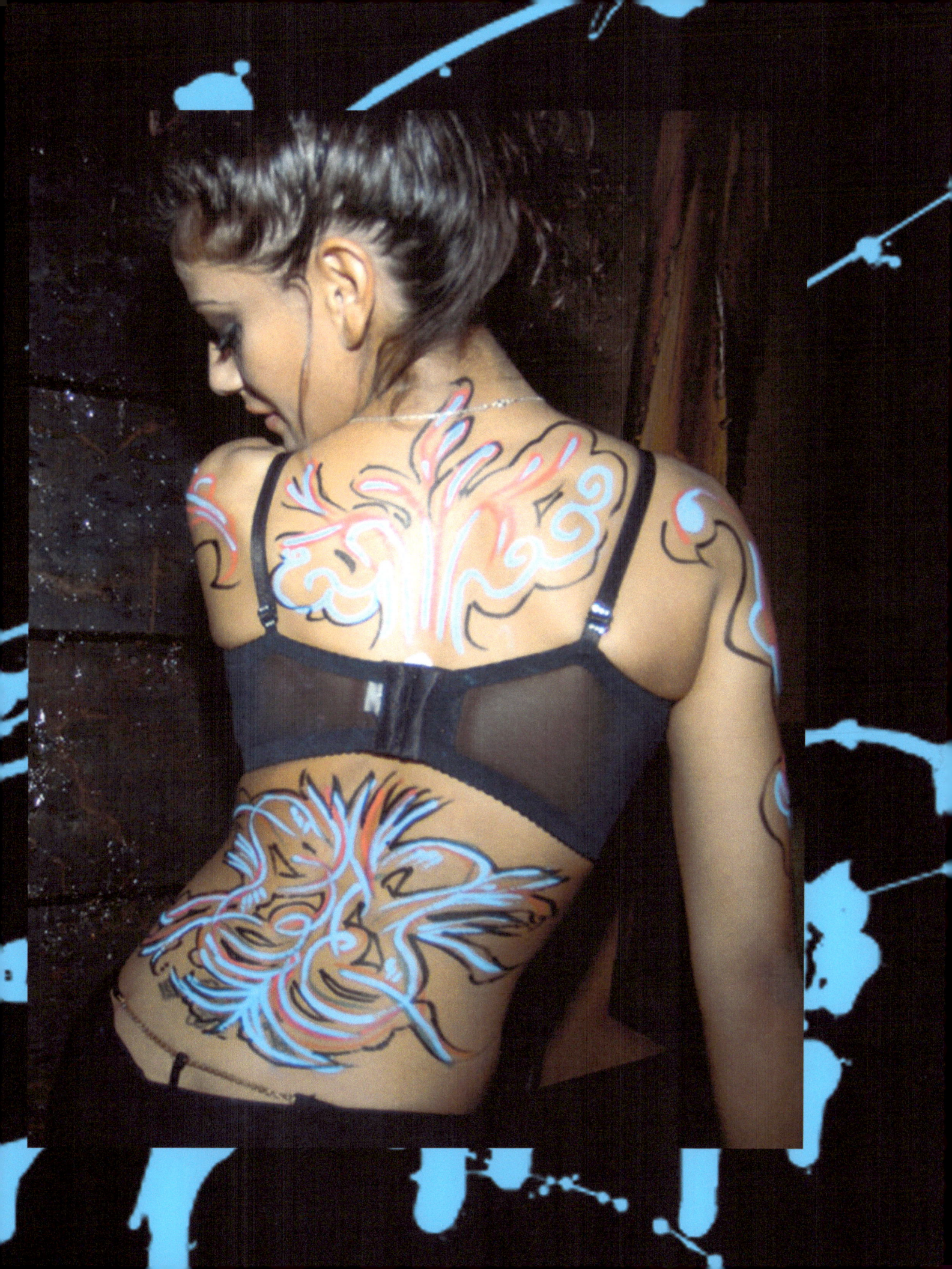

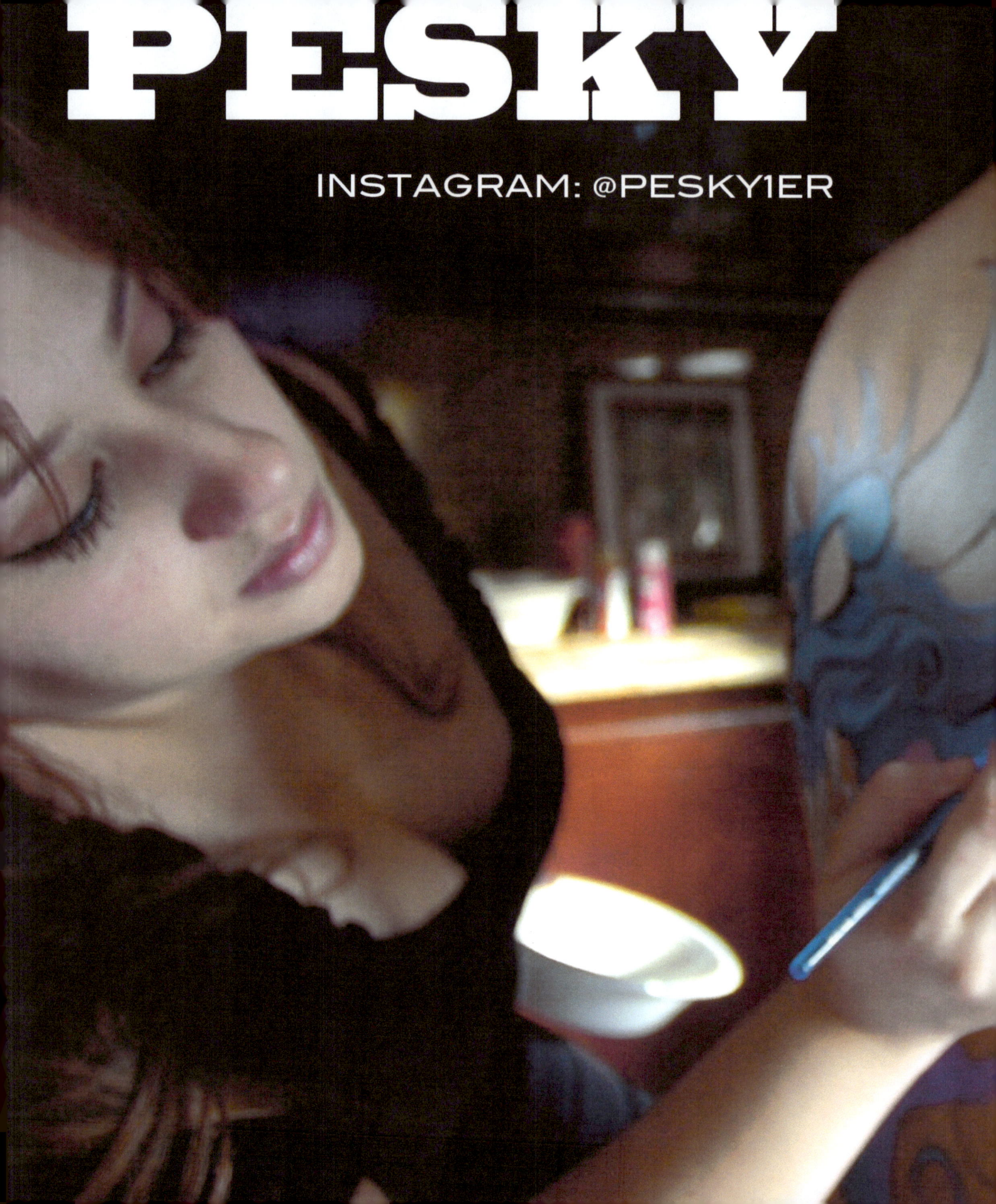

Pesky grew up in Echo Park for half of her life and then moved to Highland Park for the other half. Pesky was very influenced by her mother. She would sit and watch her mother who was studying graphic design and was always working on her art. Coming from a family of artists, by the age of five Pesky took art seriously.

    Naked Art: What kind of art do you do?

    Pesky: Drawing, sketches, spray painting, murals, body art, sculpting, crafts, paintings.

    NA: How long have you been doing body art and how did you get into it?

    Pesky: In 2008, I got approached to do body art and then people wanted female body painters so they would call me.

    NA: How is body painting different from the other art you do?

    Pesky: You can keep a canvas but body art washes right off, but the pics are cool. It's also fun because you talk to the model unlike painting on a canvas where it's more lonely.

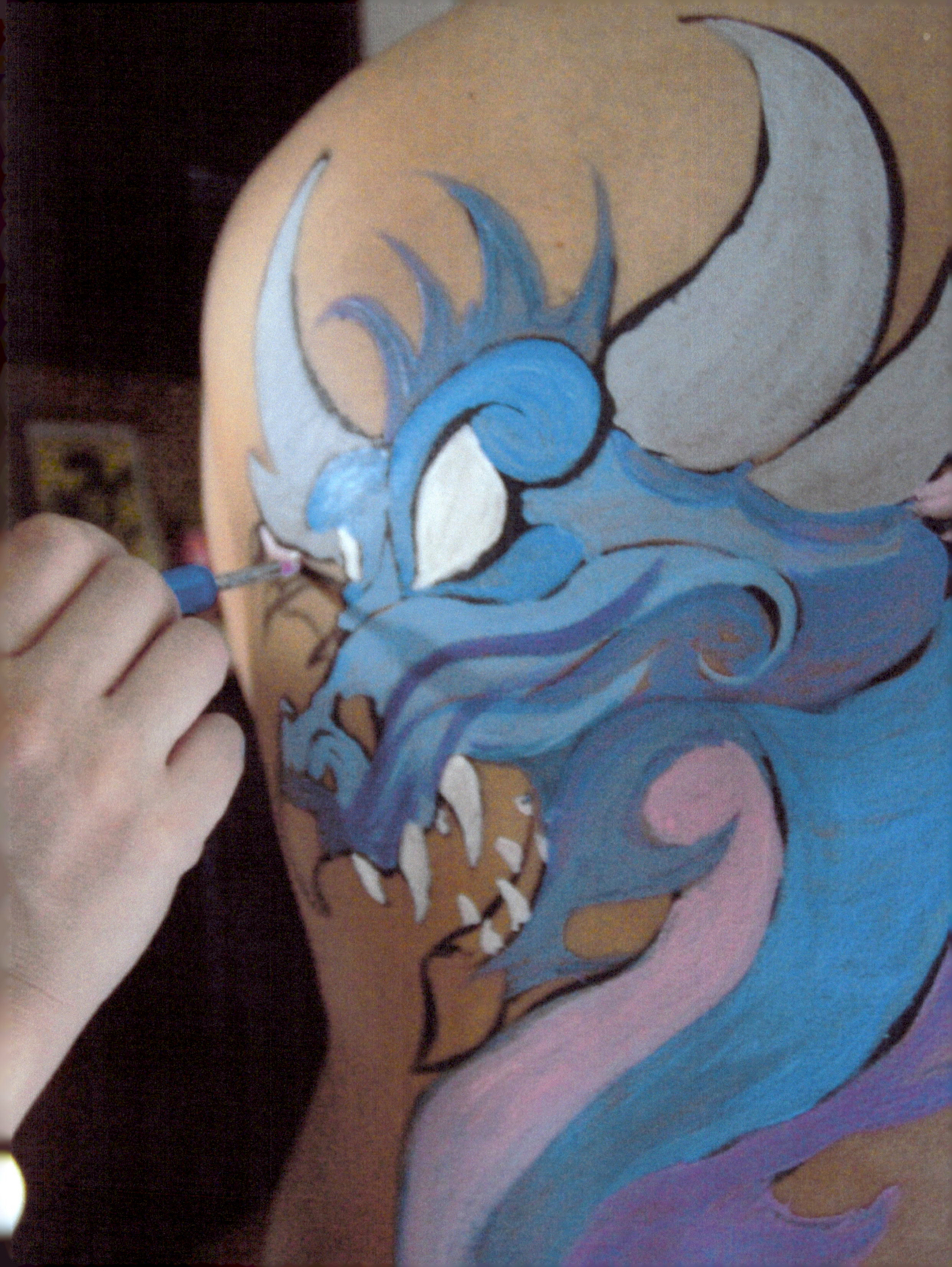

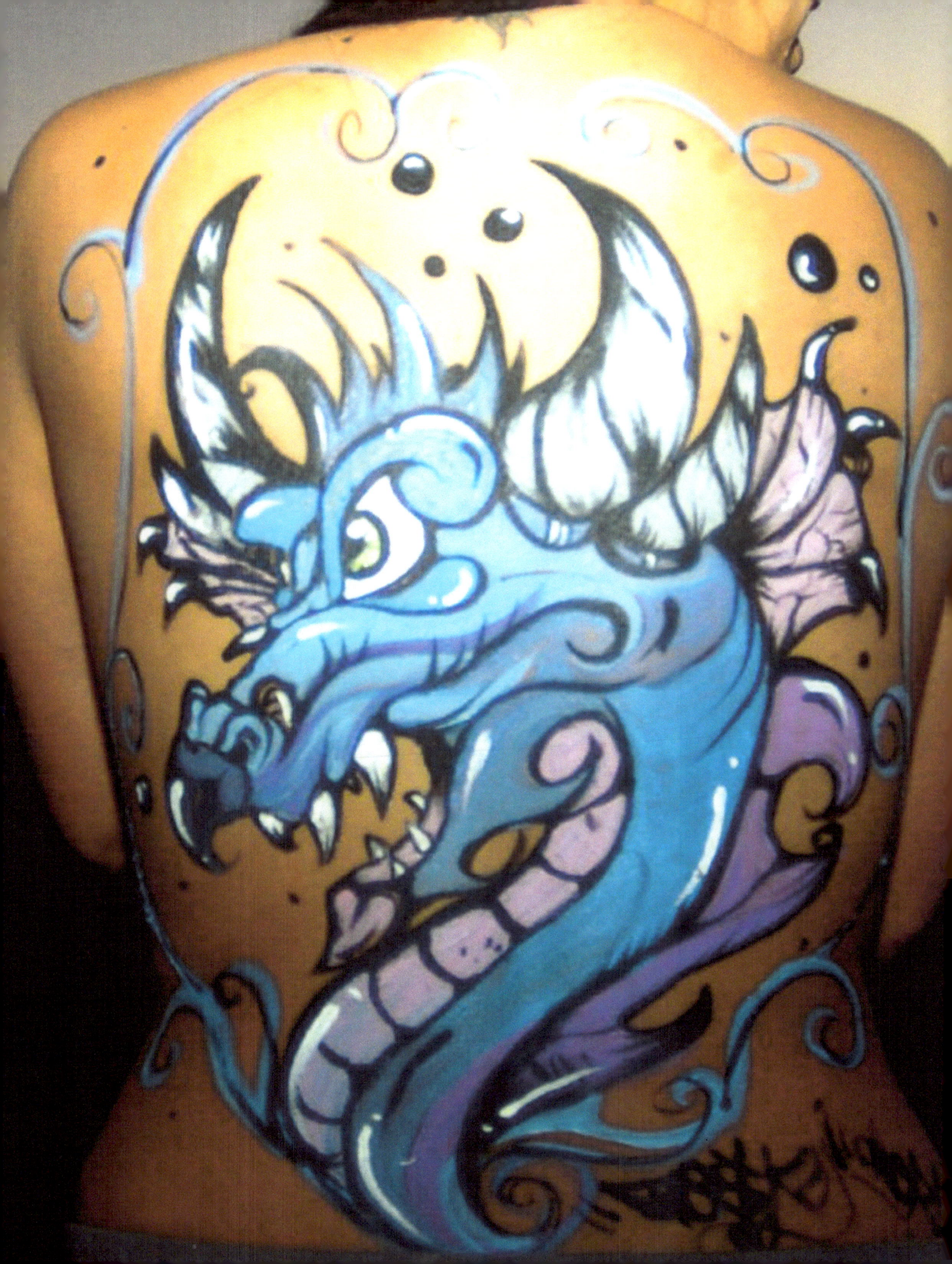

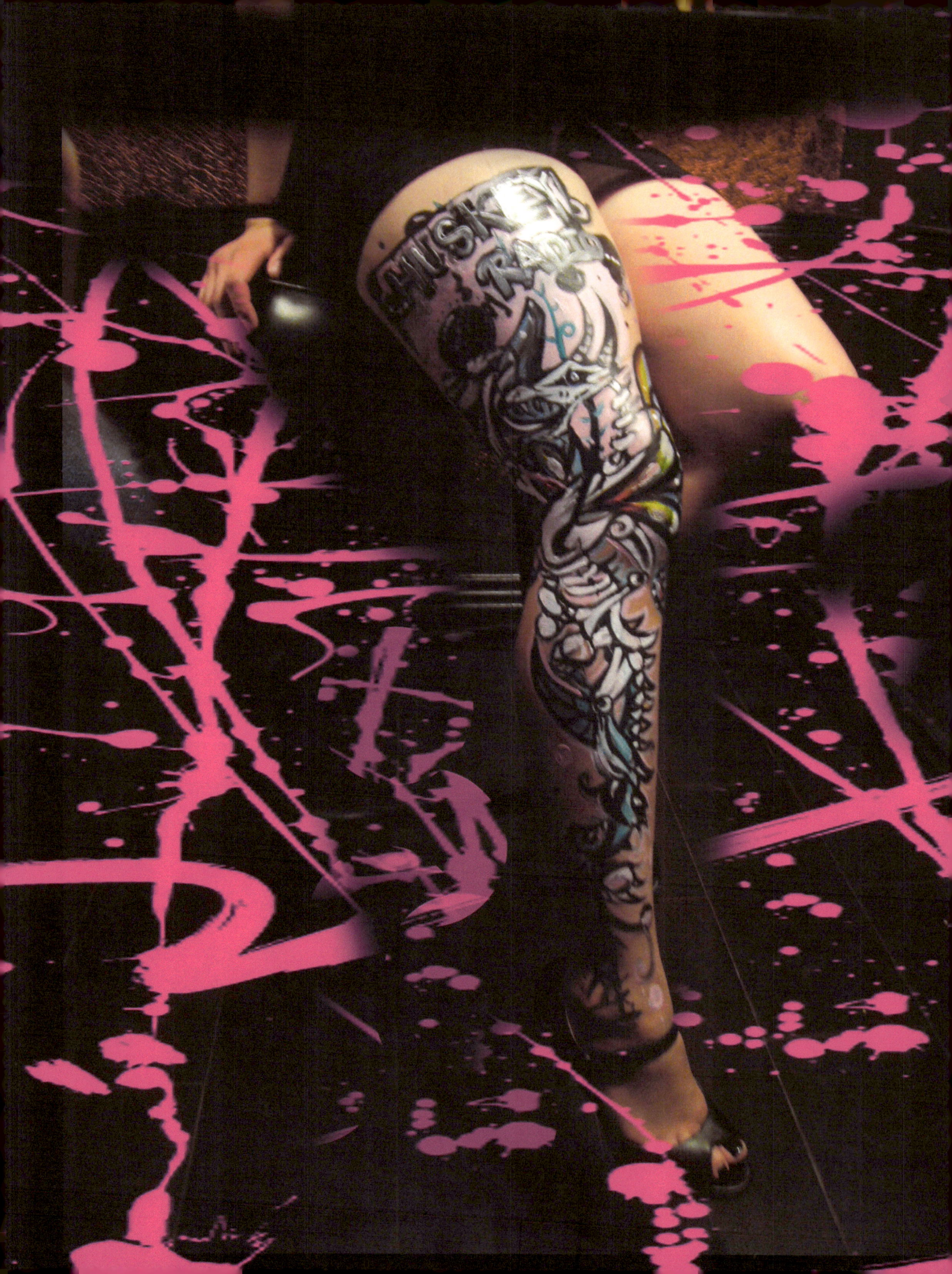

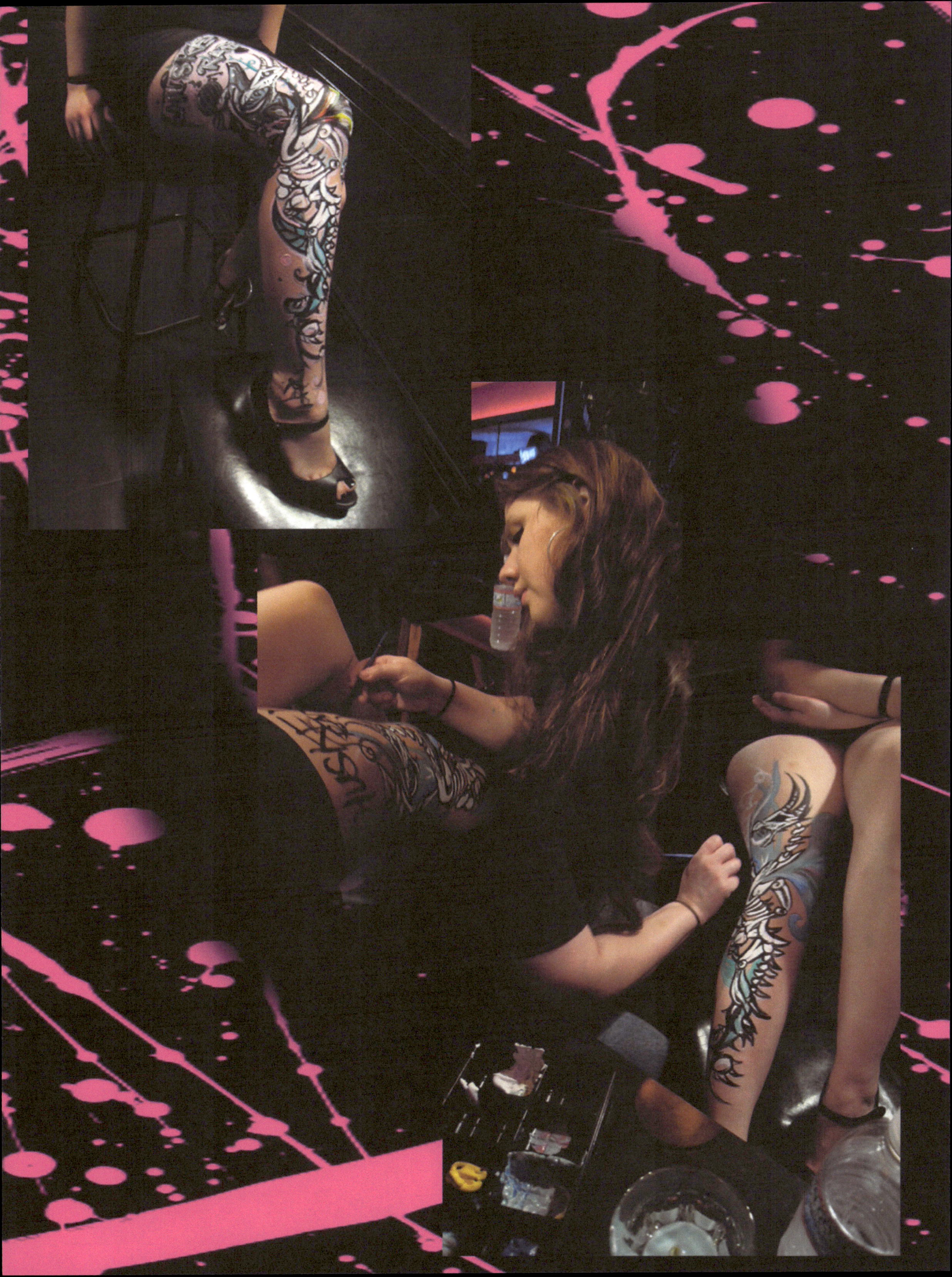

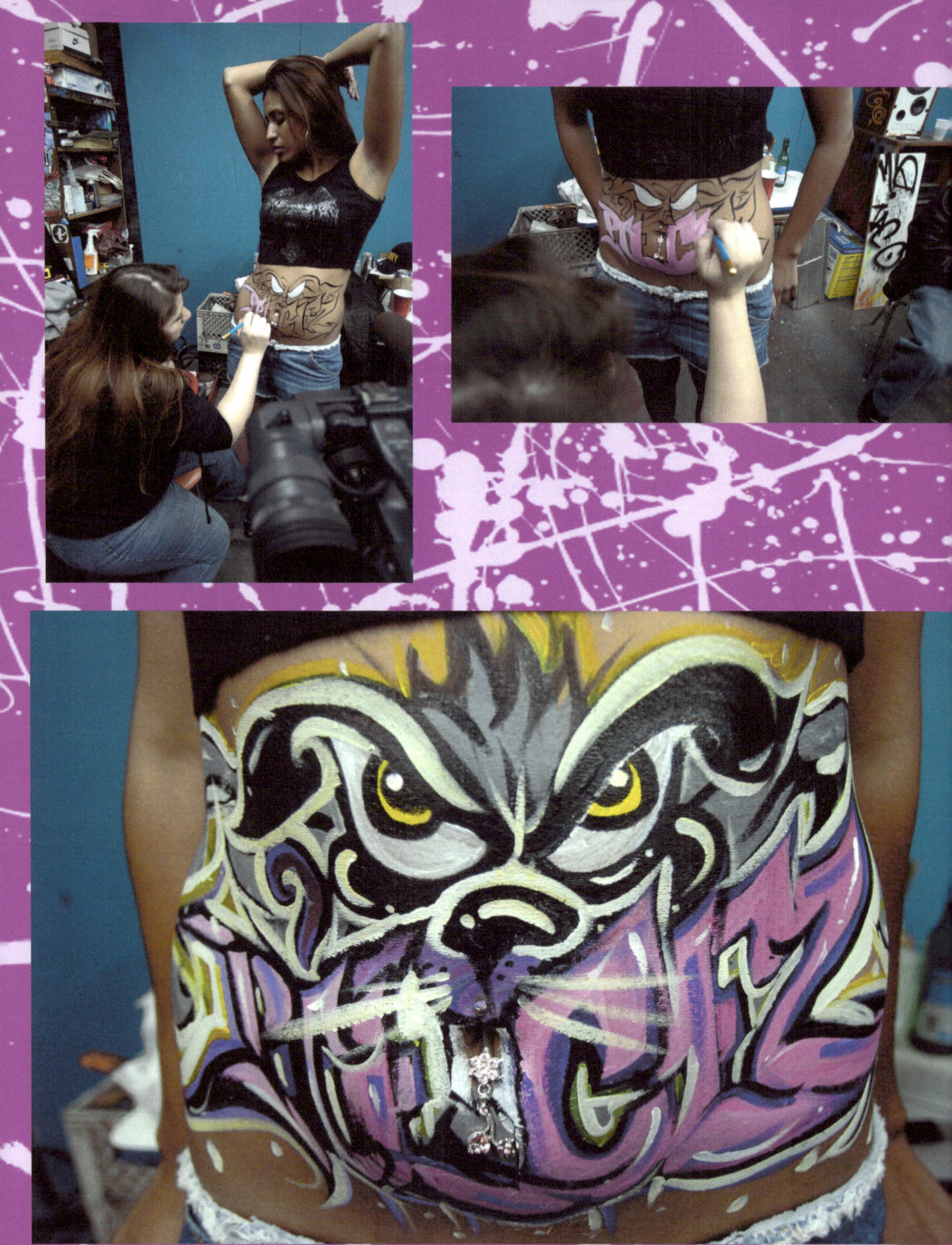

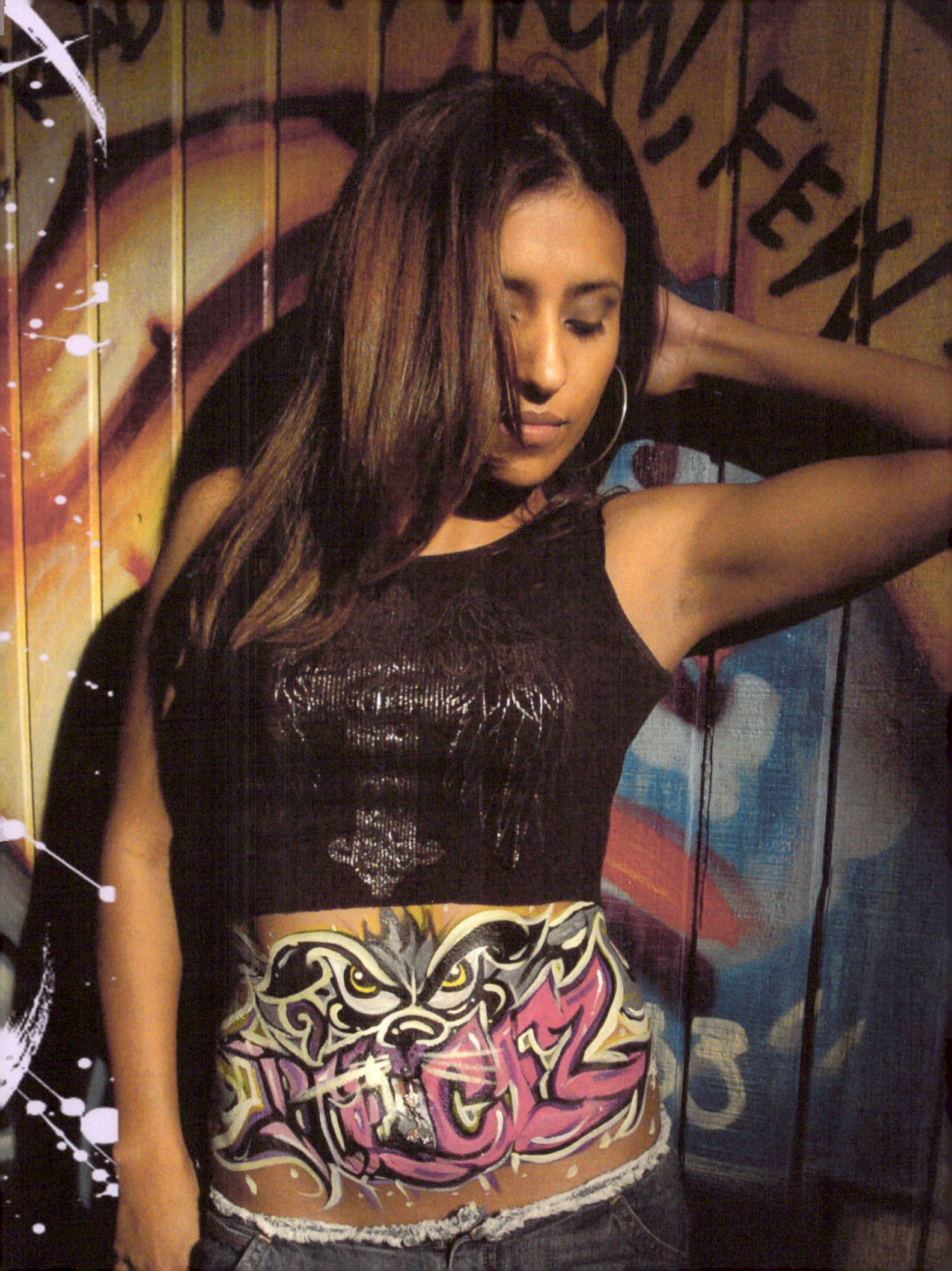

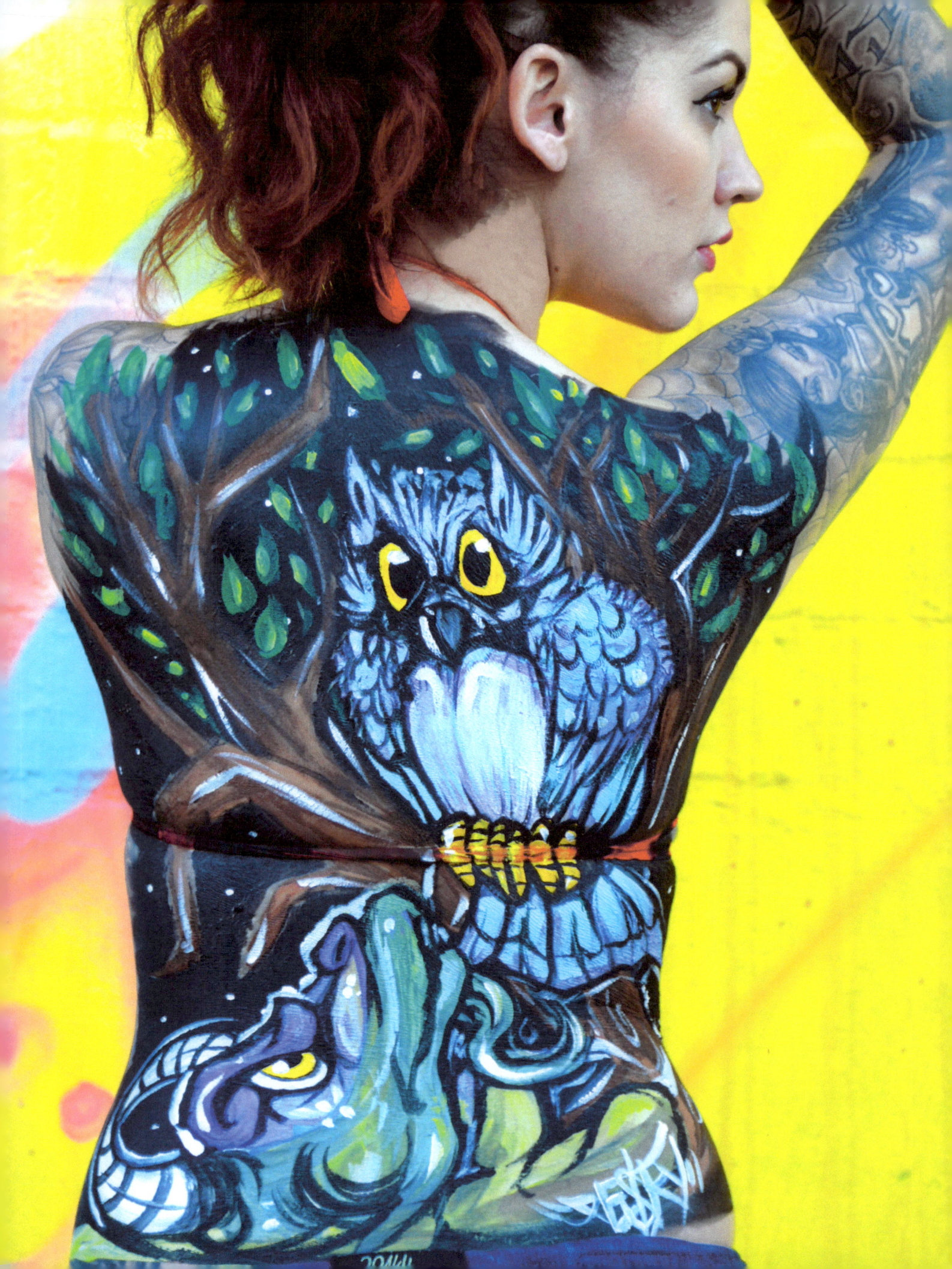

INSTAGRAM: @MIGONE2013

MIG ONE

was born in Nicargua and raised in North East Los Angeles. He has been drawing since the age of 12. He went from spray painting walls to mastering various fields of art such as airbrush, graphic design, sign and logo development, silkscreen, and body art.

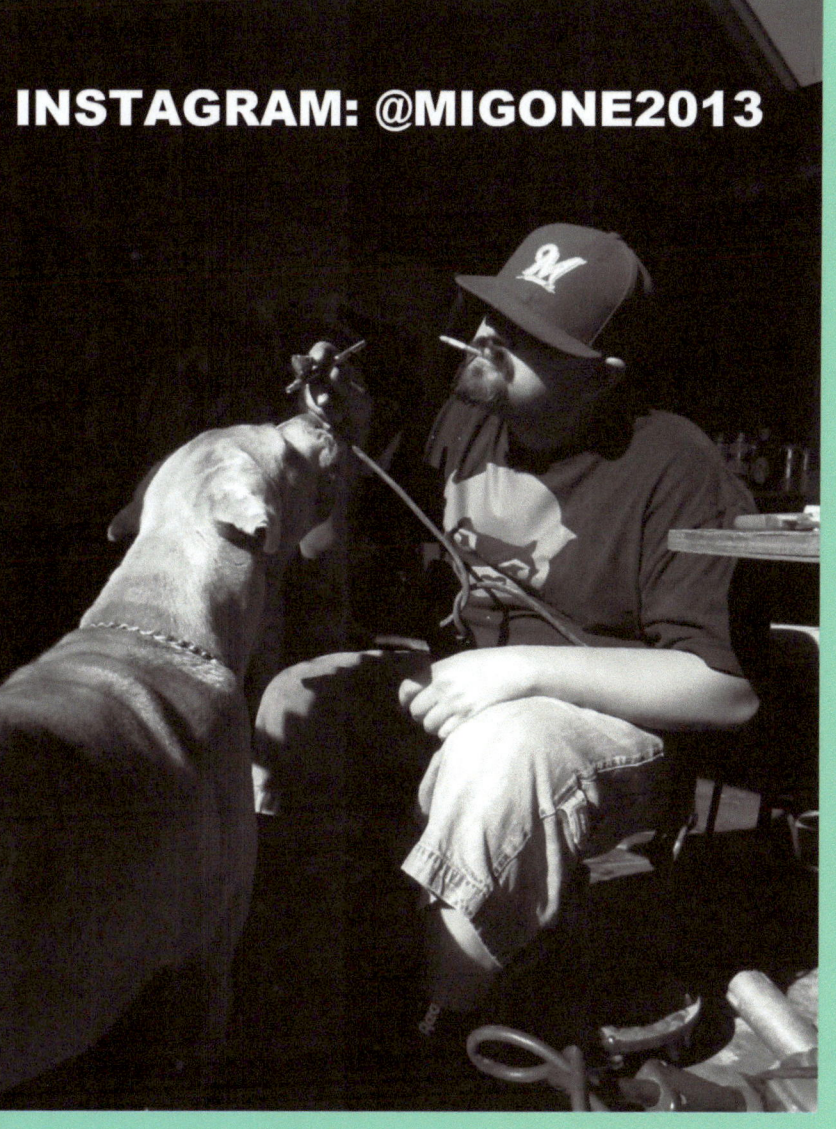

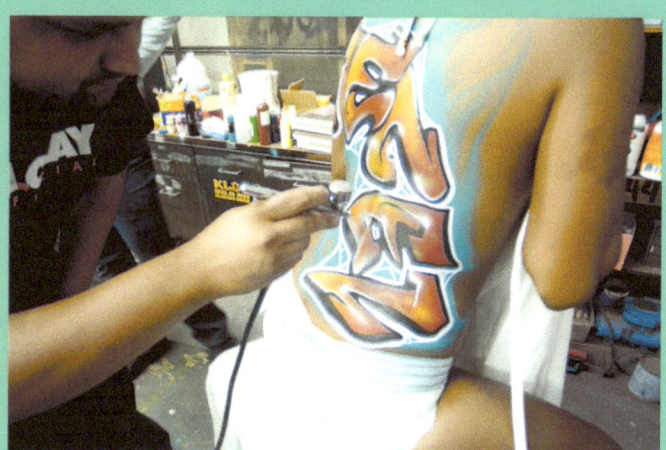

NA: How long have you been doing body art?

Mig: Since 2007.

NA: In the seven years of doing body art how has your style developed?

Mig: I've learned that there are diferent paints for different effects. I use Diamond FX for brush work on the body and I use Vibe paint for airbrush work.

NA: What do you like about doing body art?

Mig: It's a different media. You have to do it on the spot, not like a canvas. It's more challenging and that's better. Plus, body art looks great on the beautiful women.

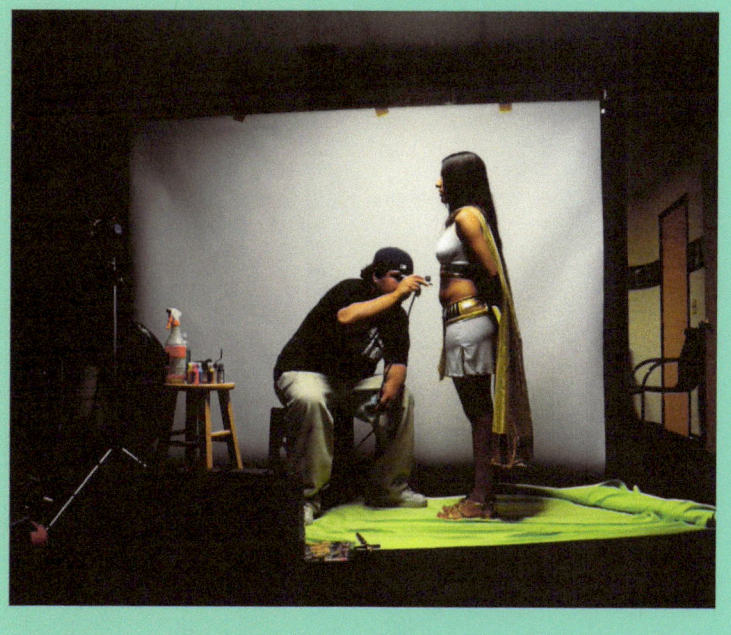

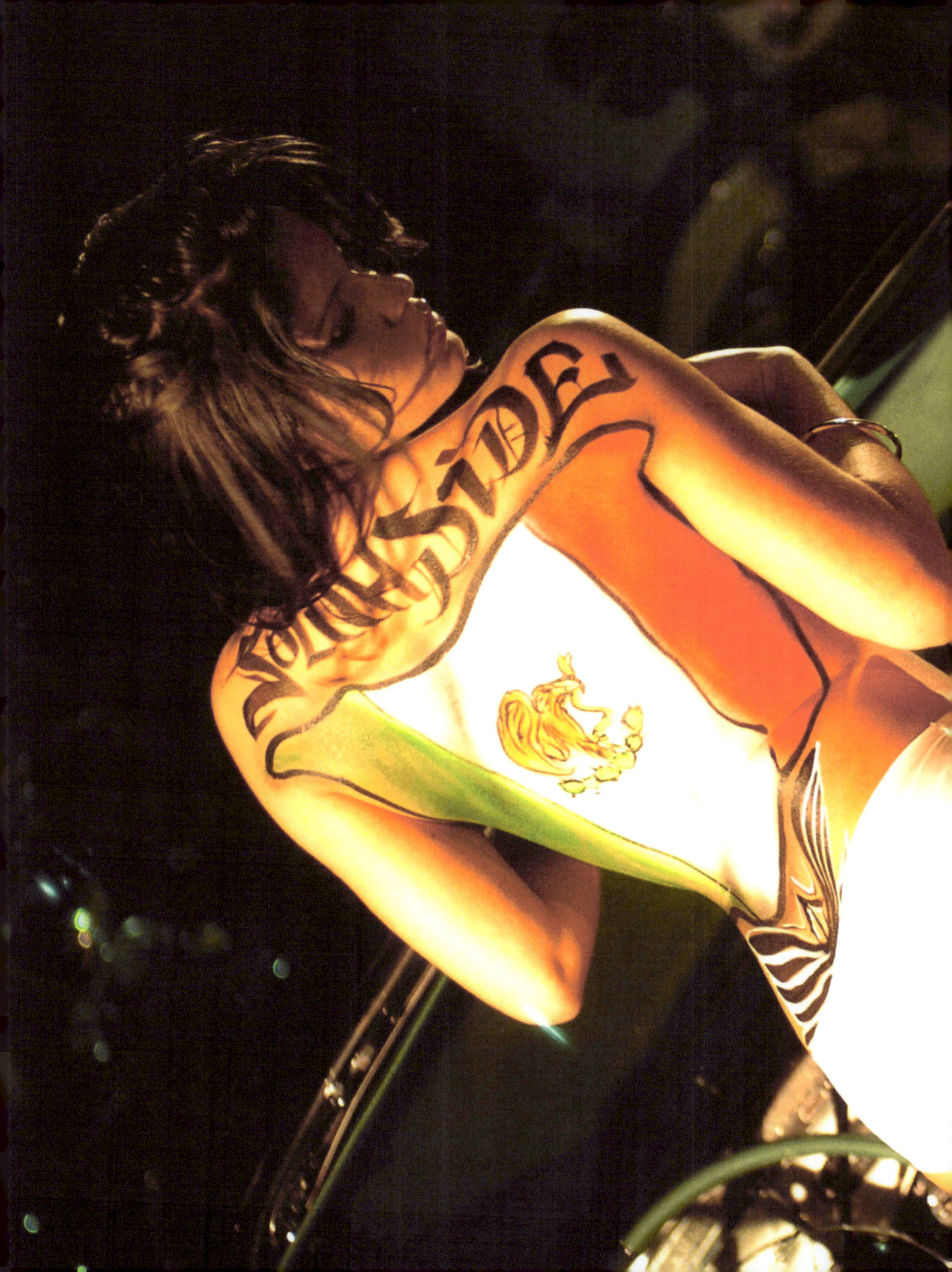

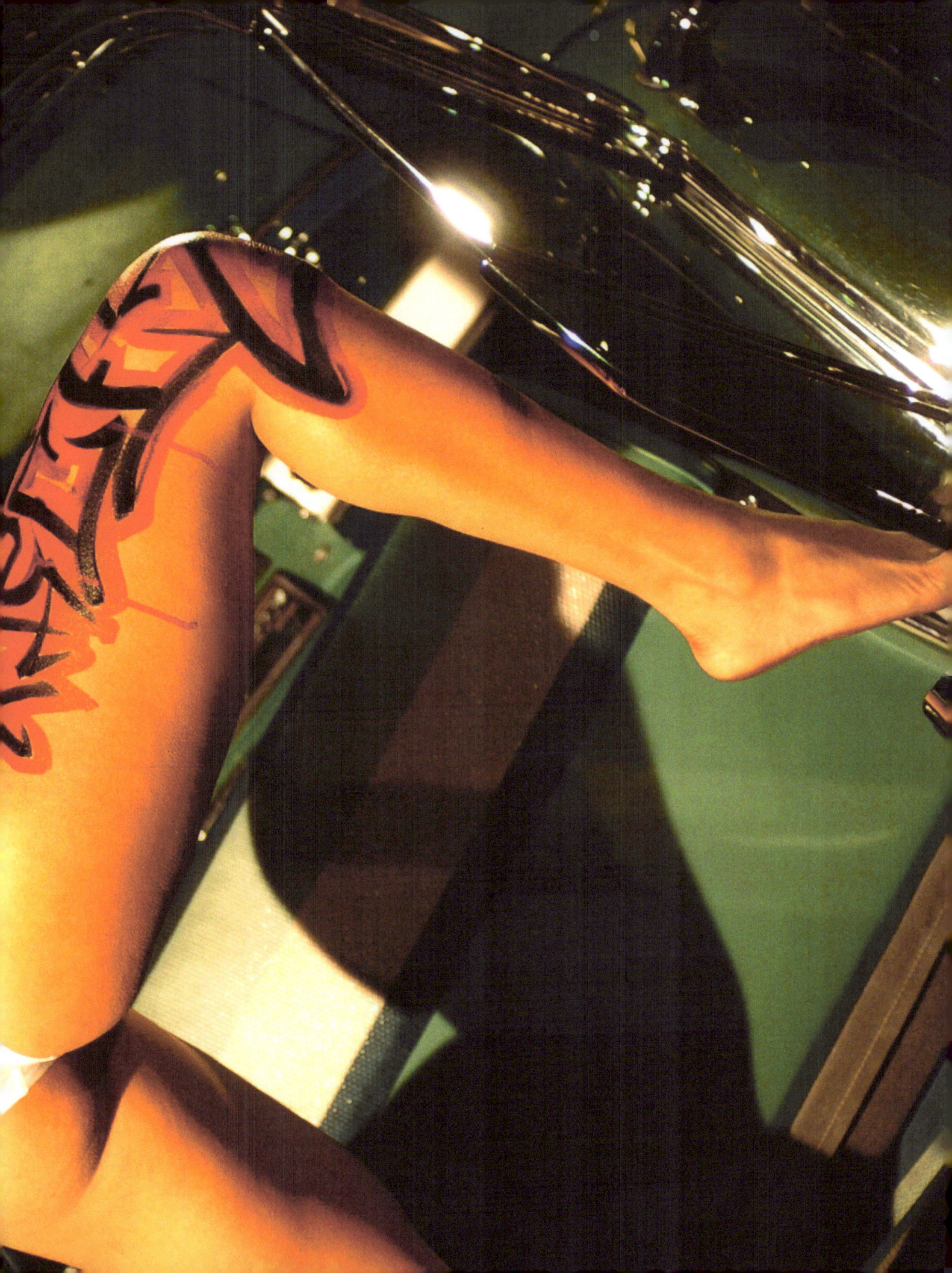

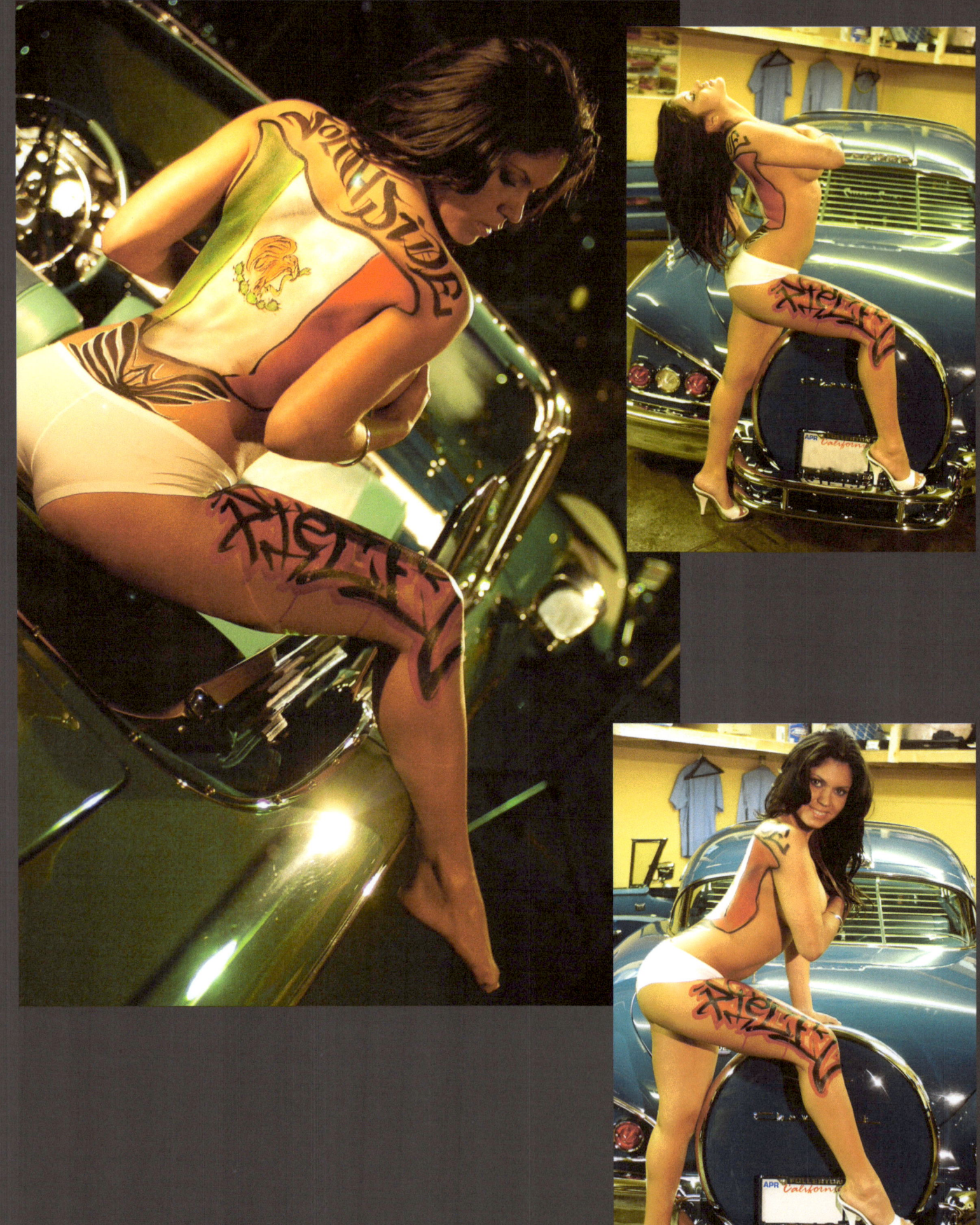

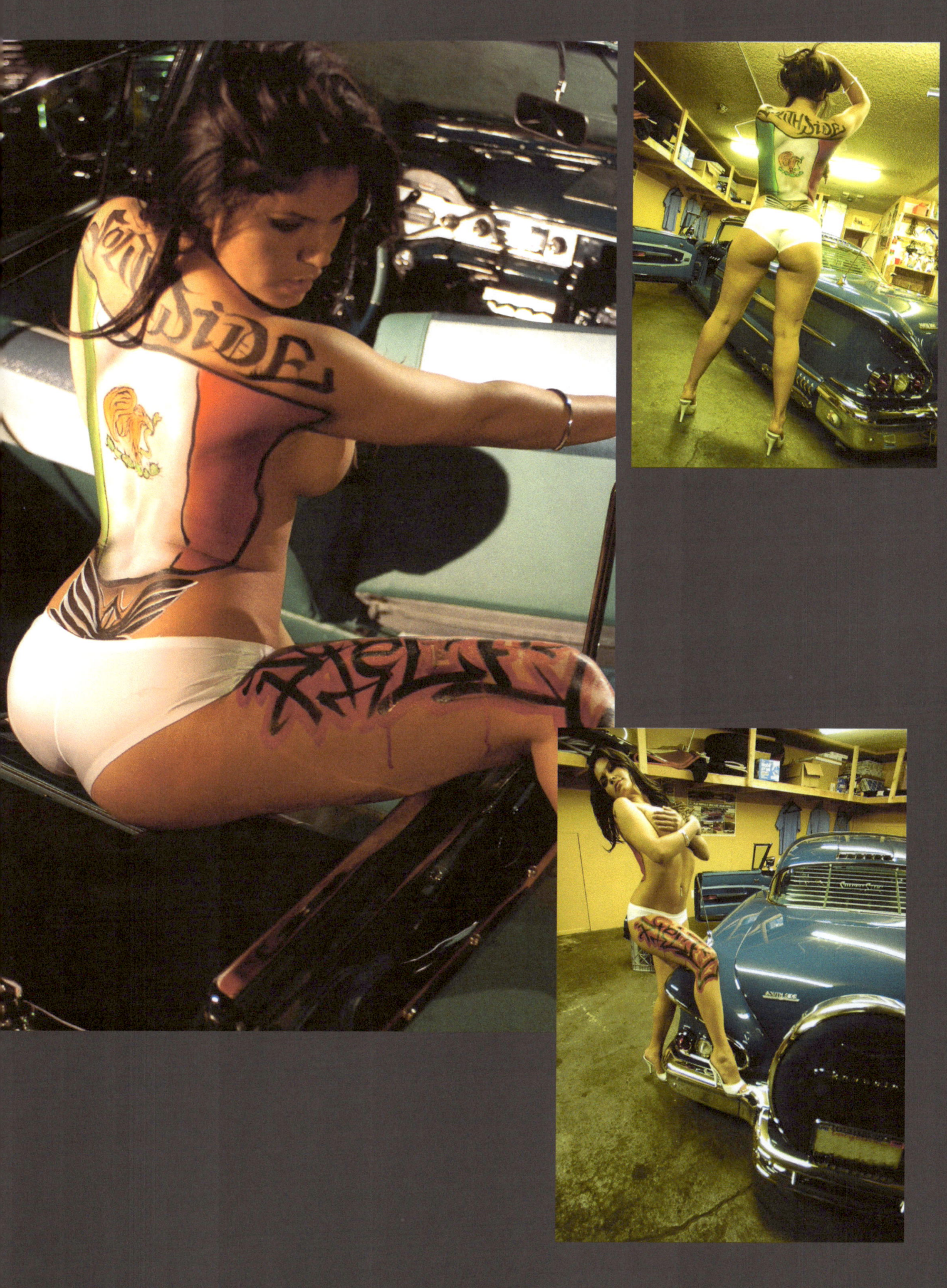

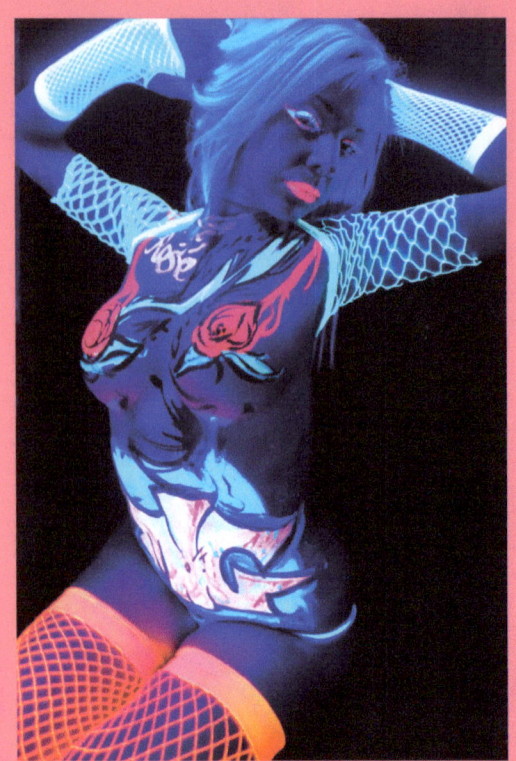
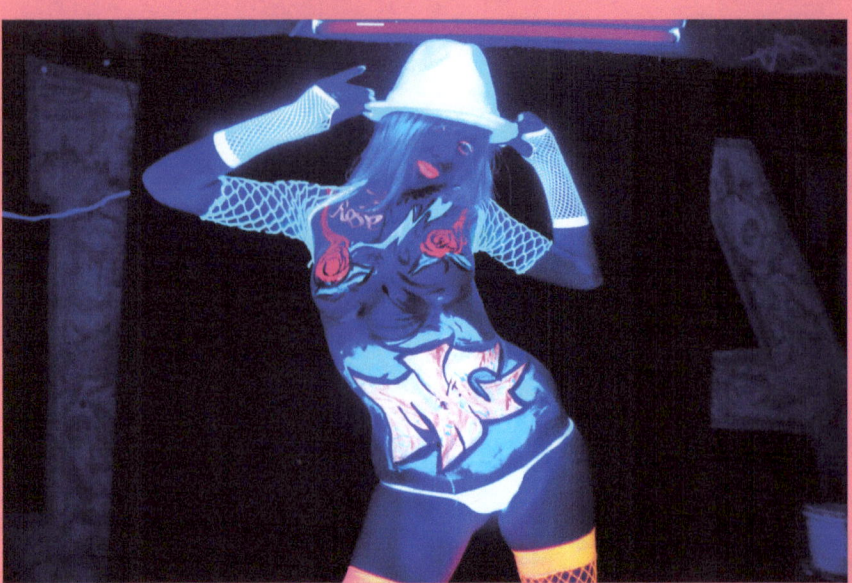
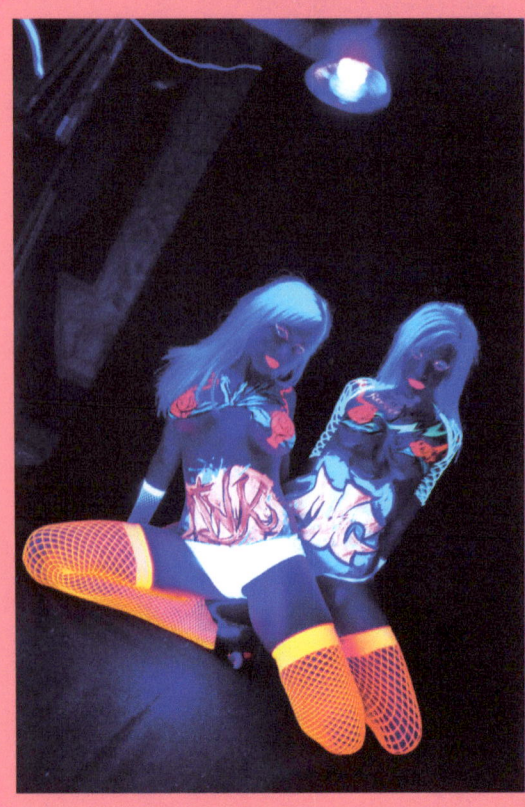

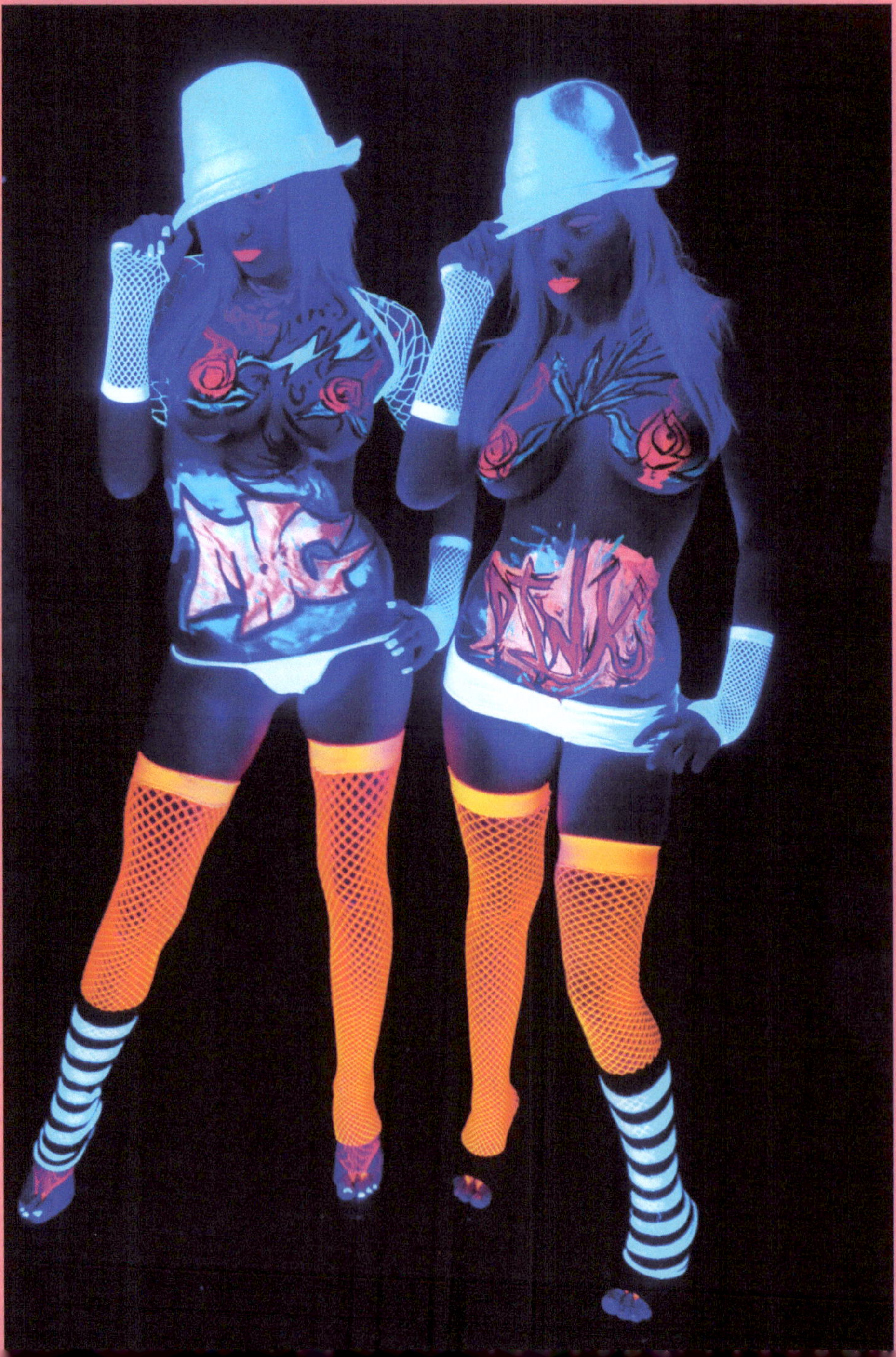

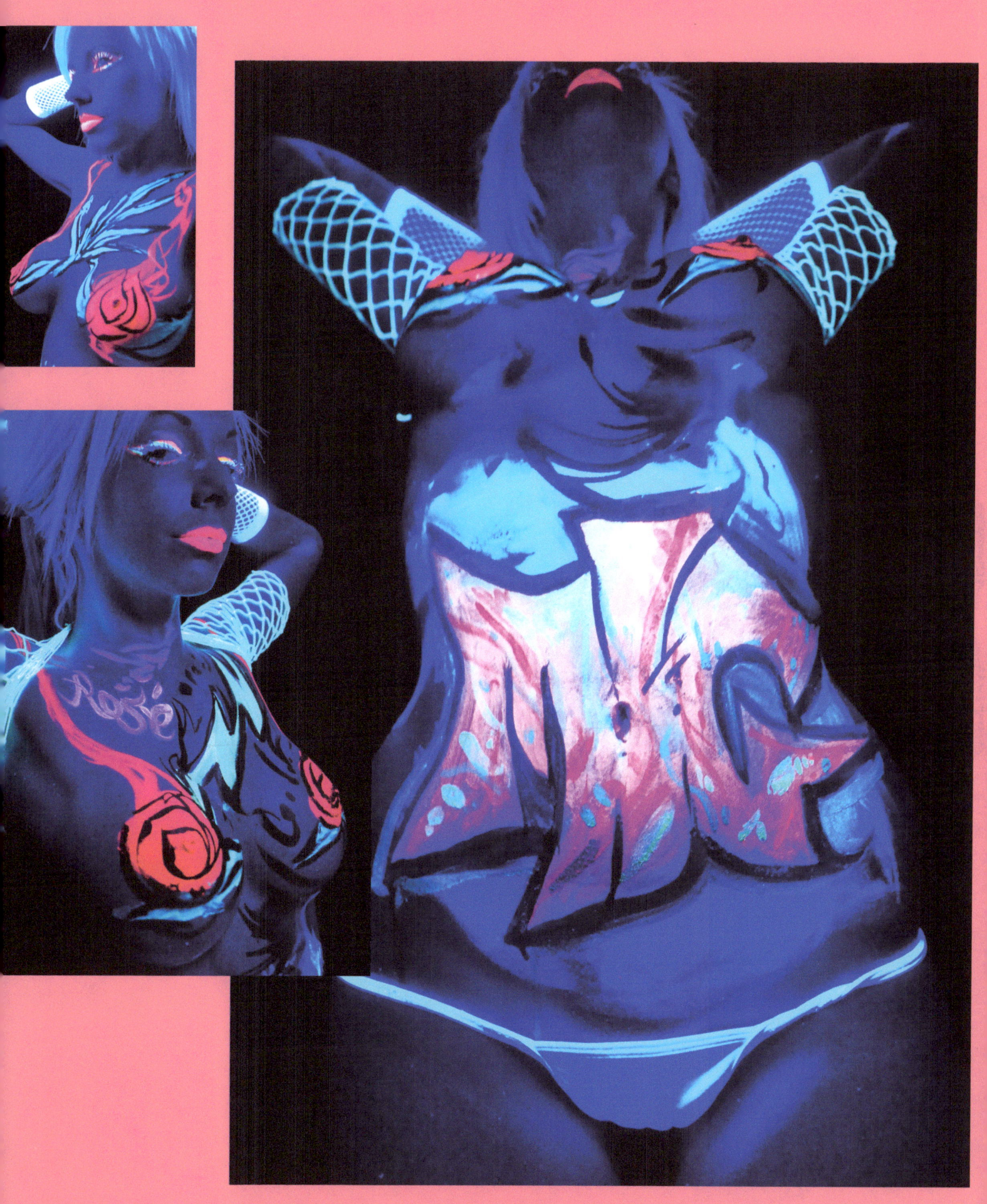

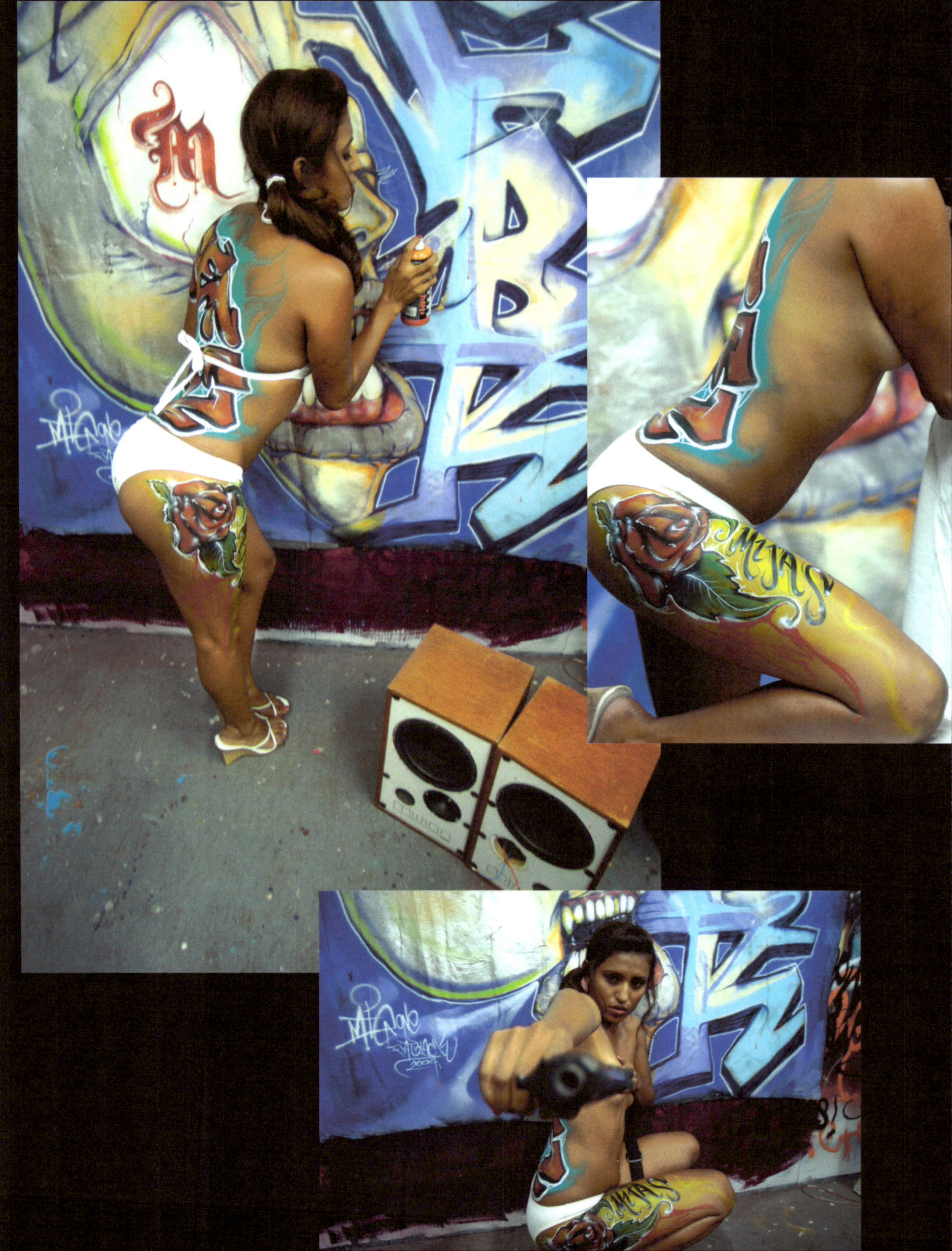

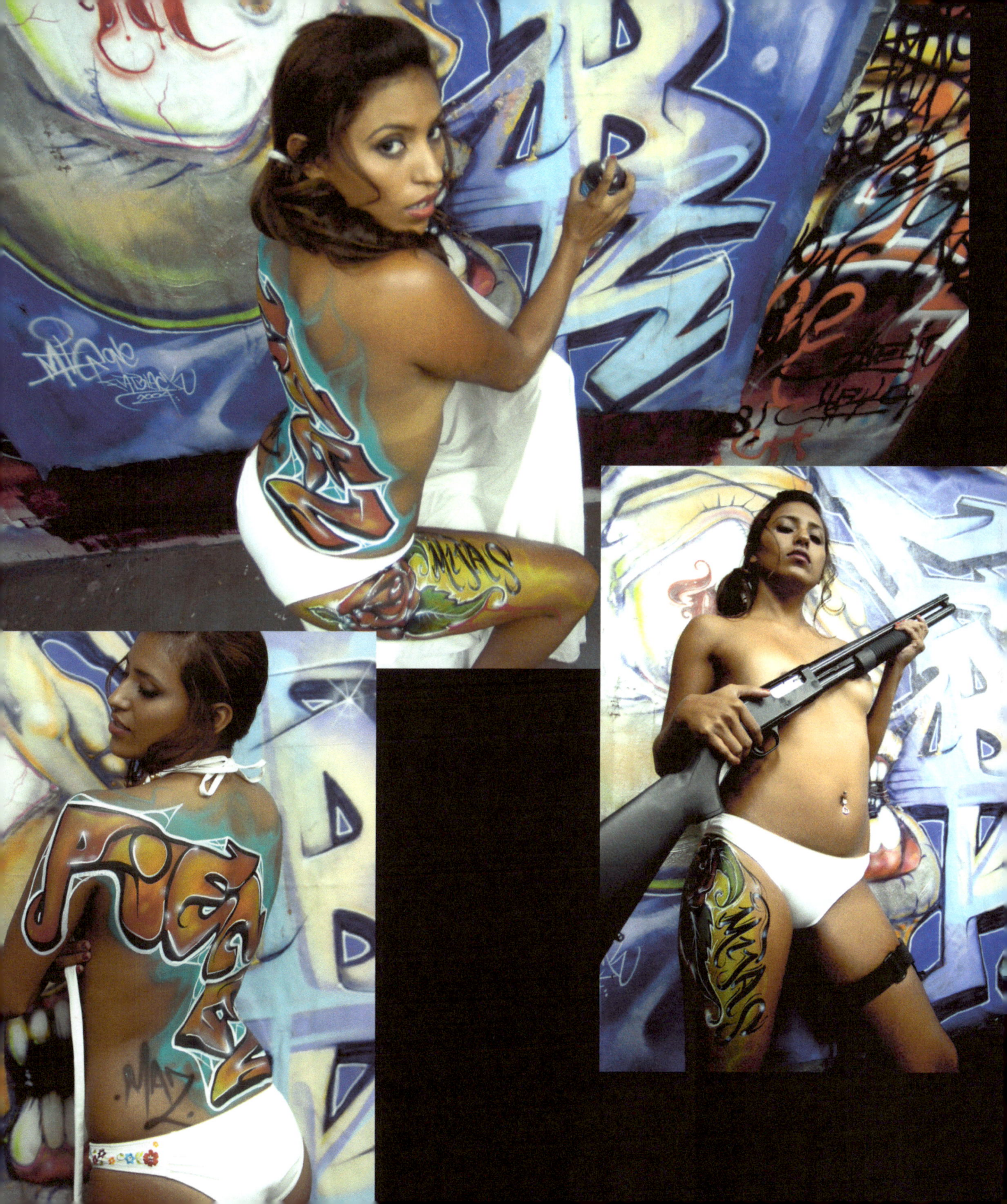

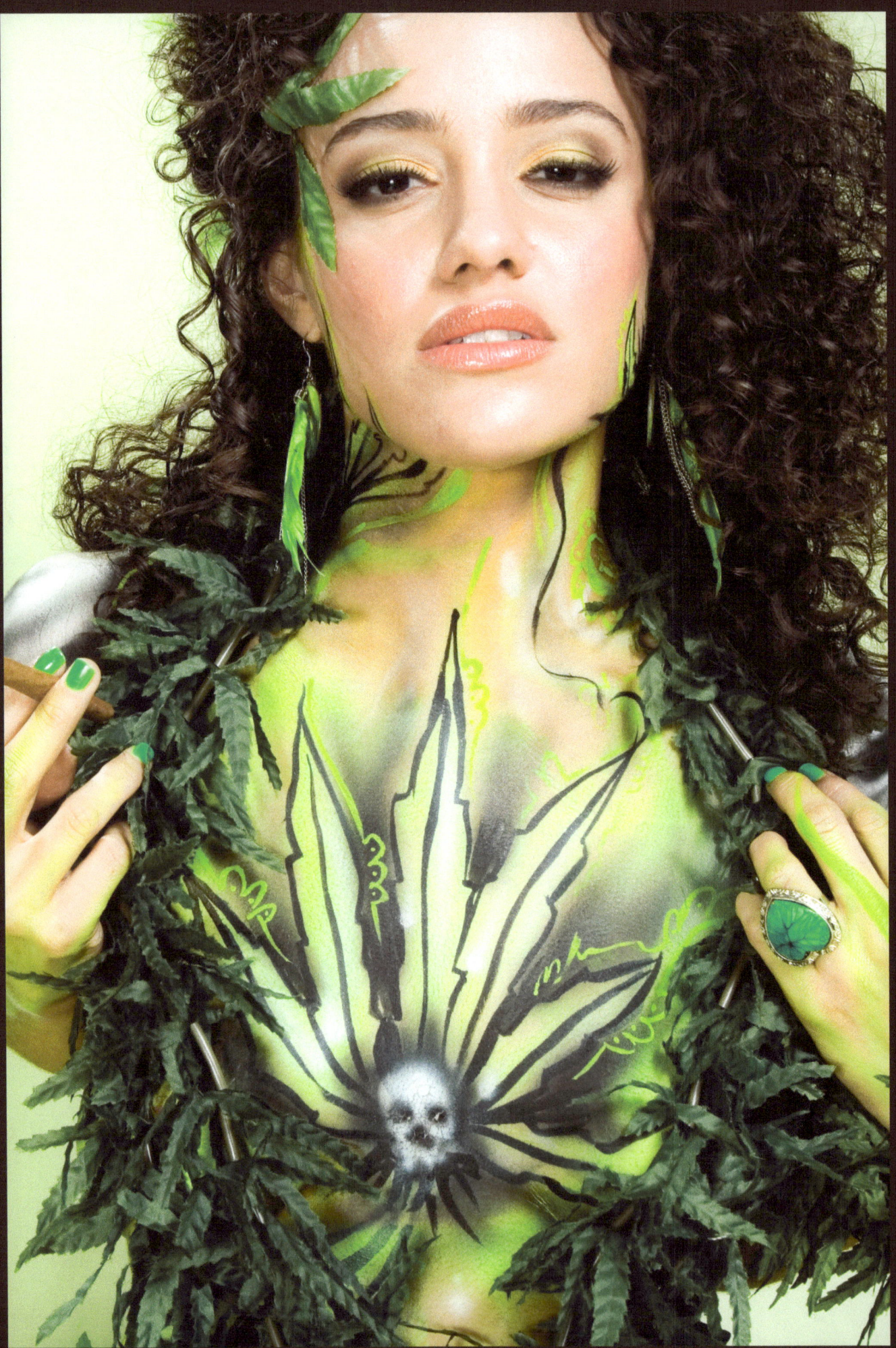

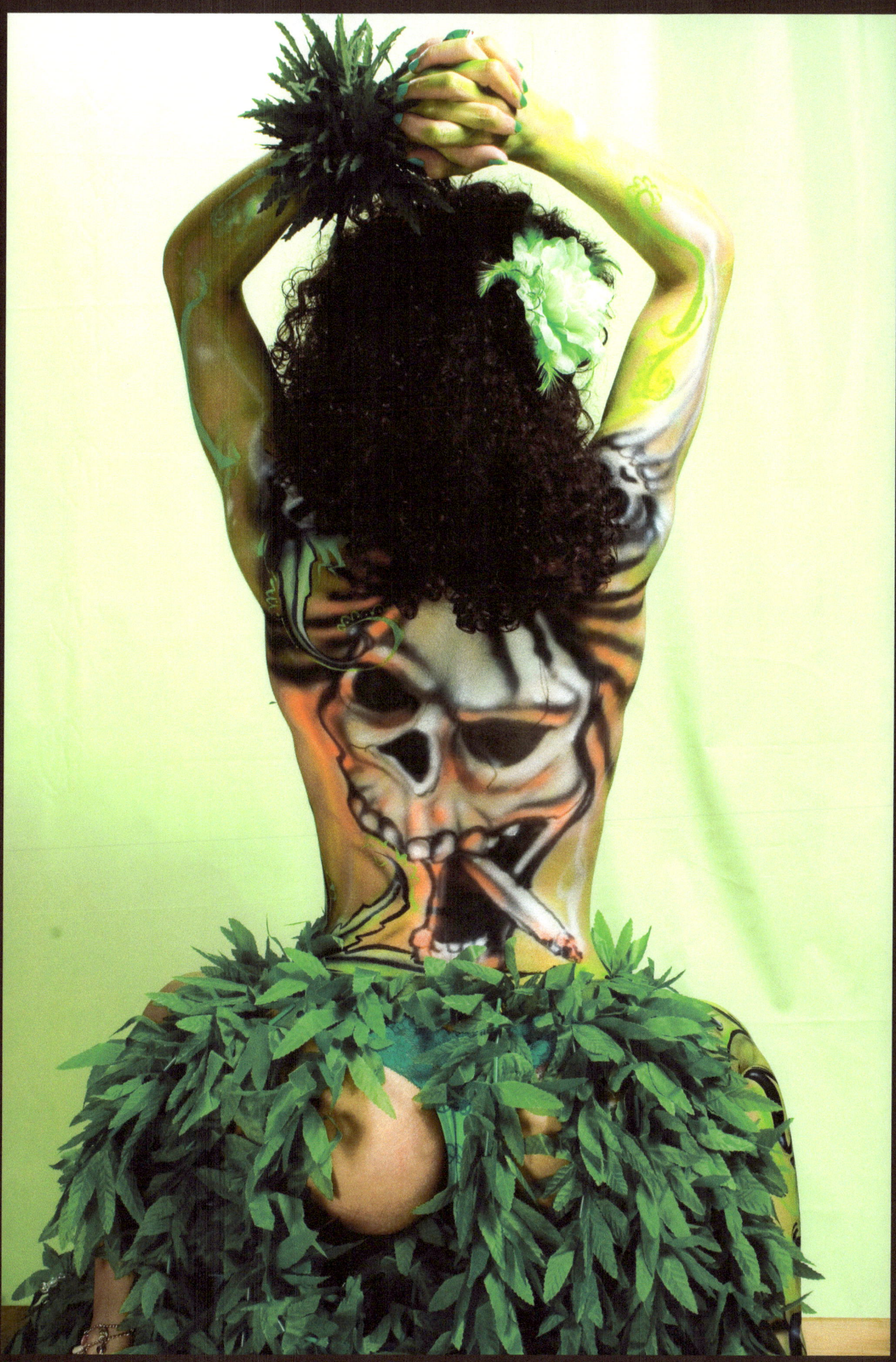

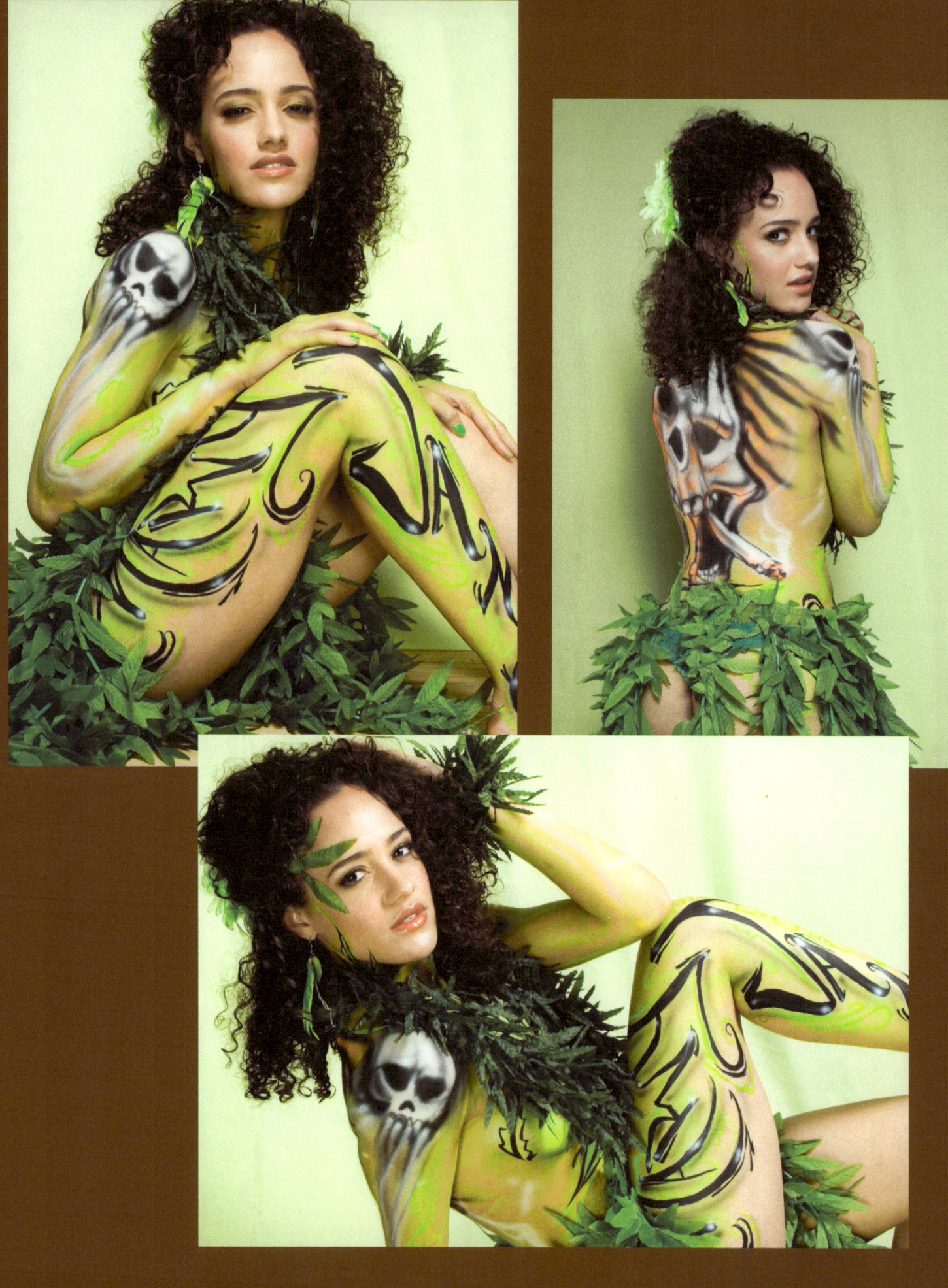

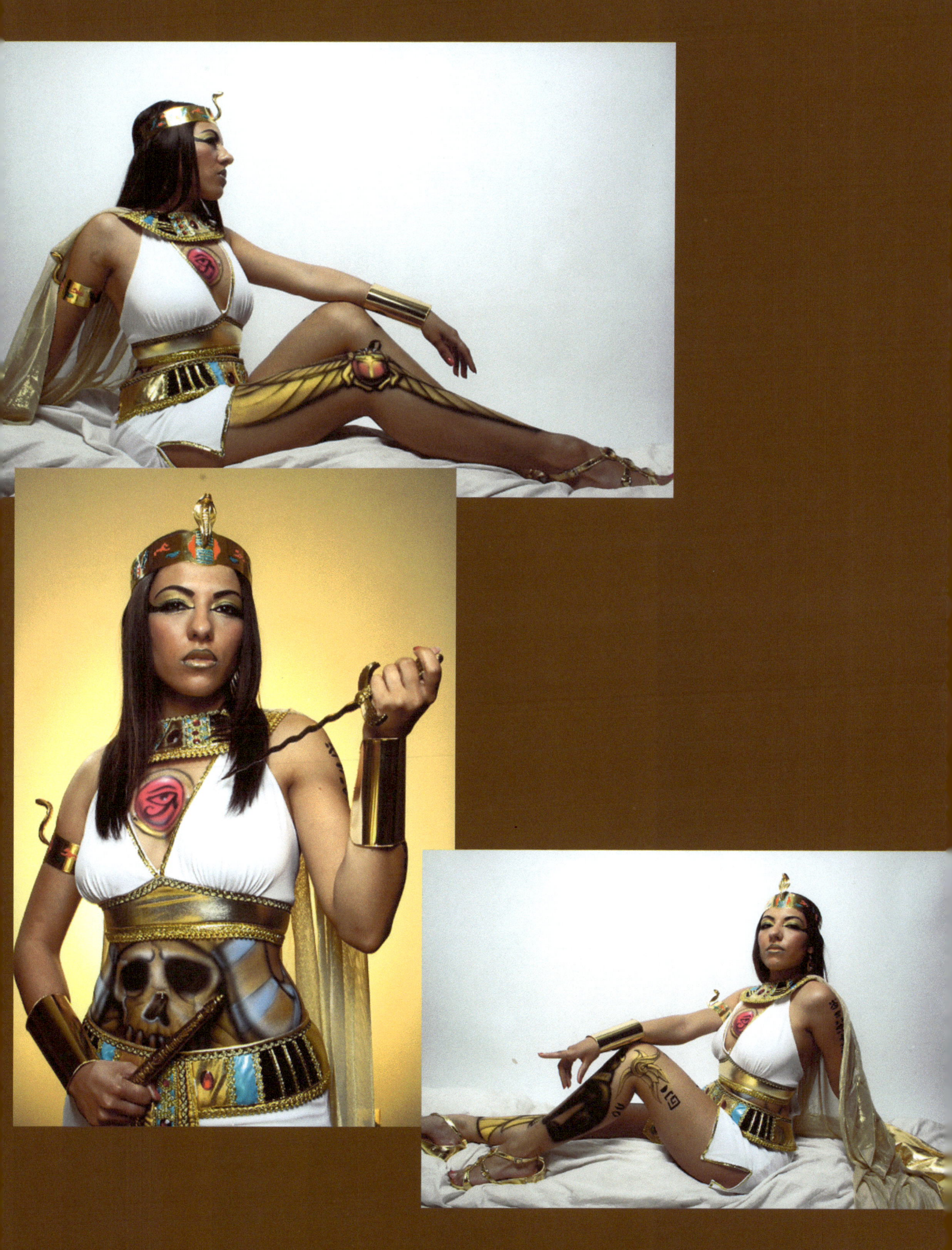

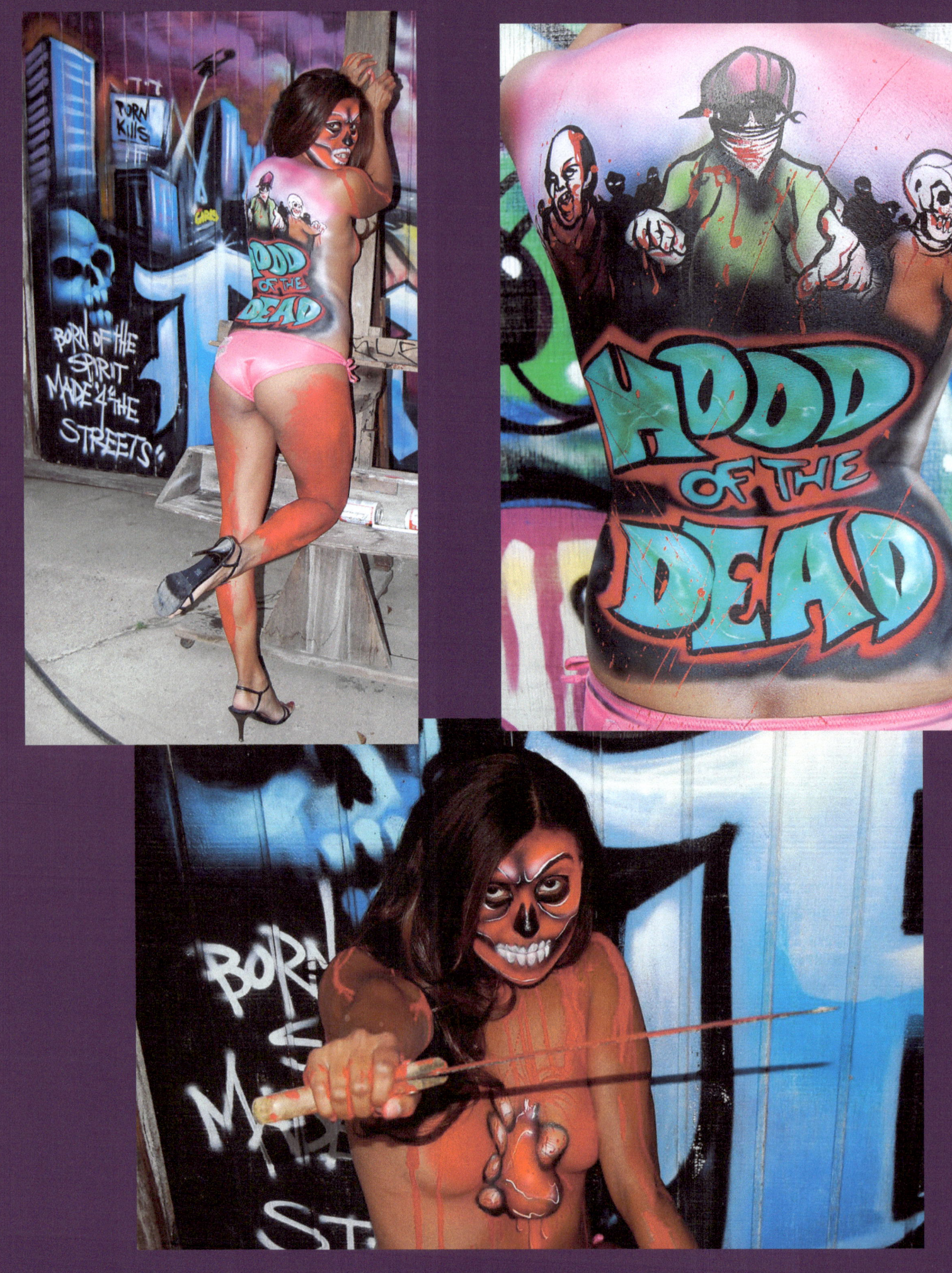

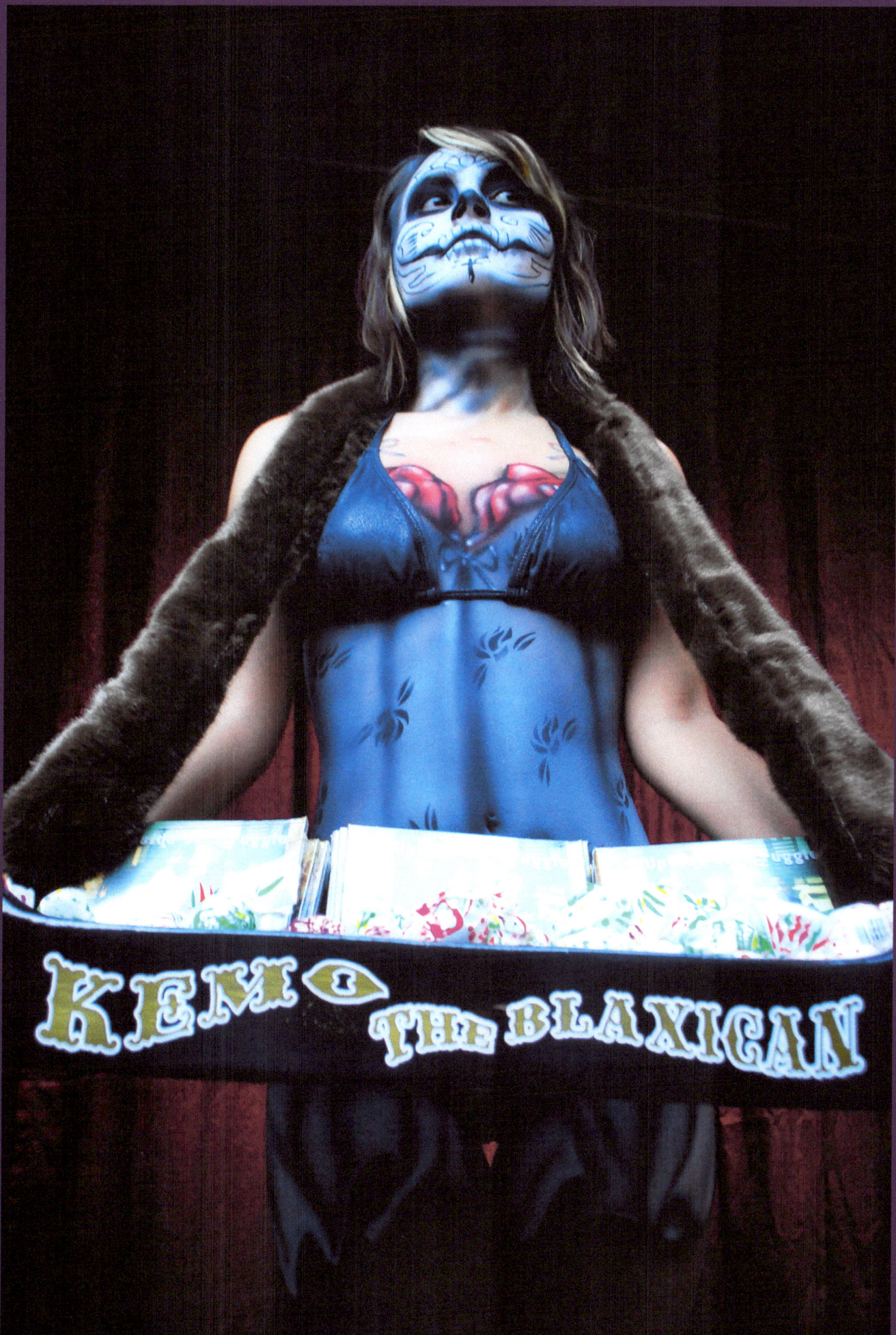

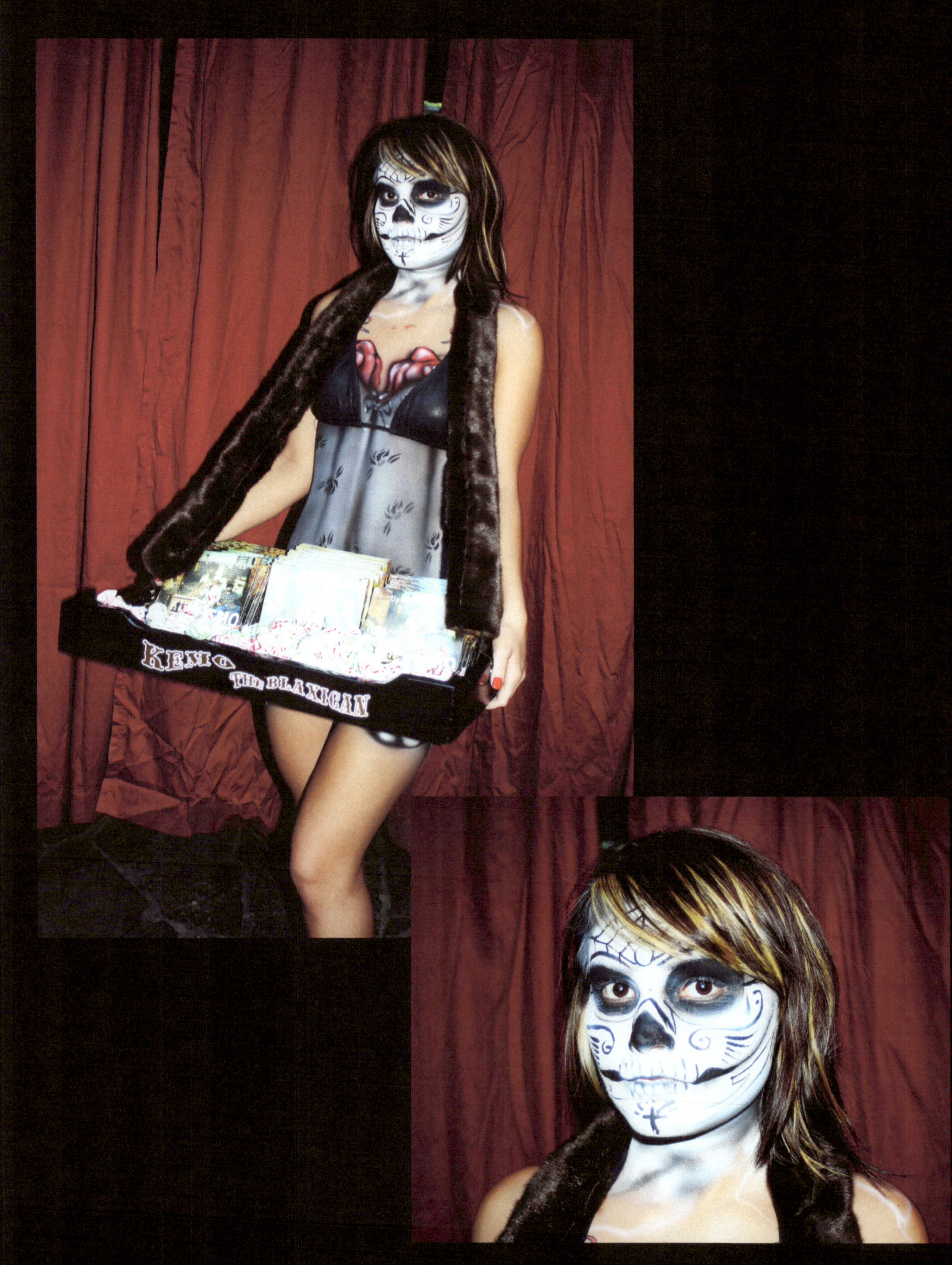

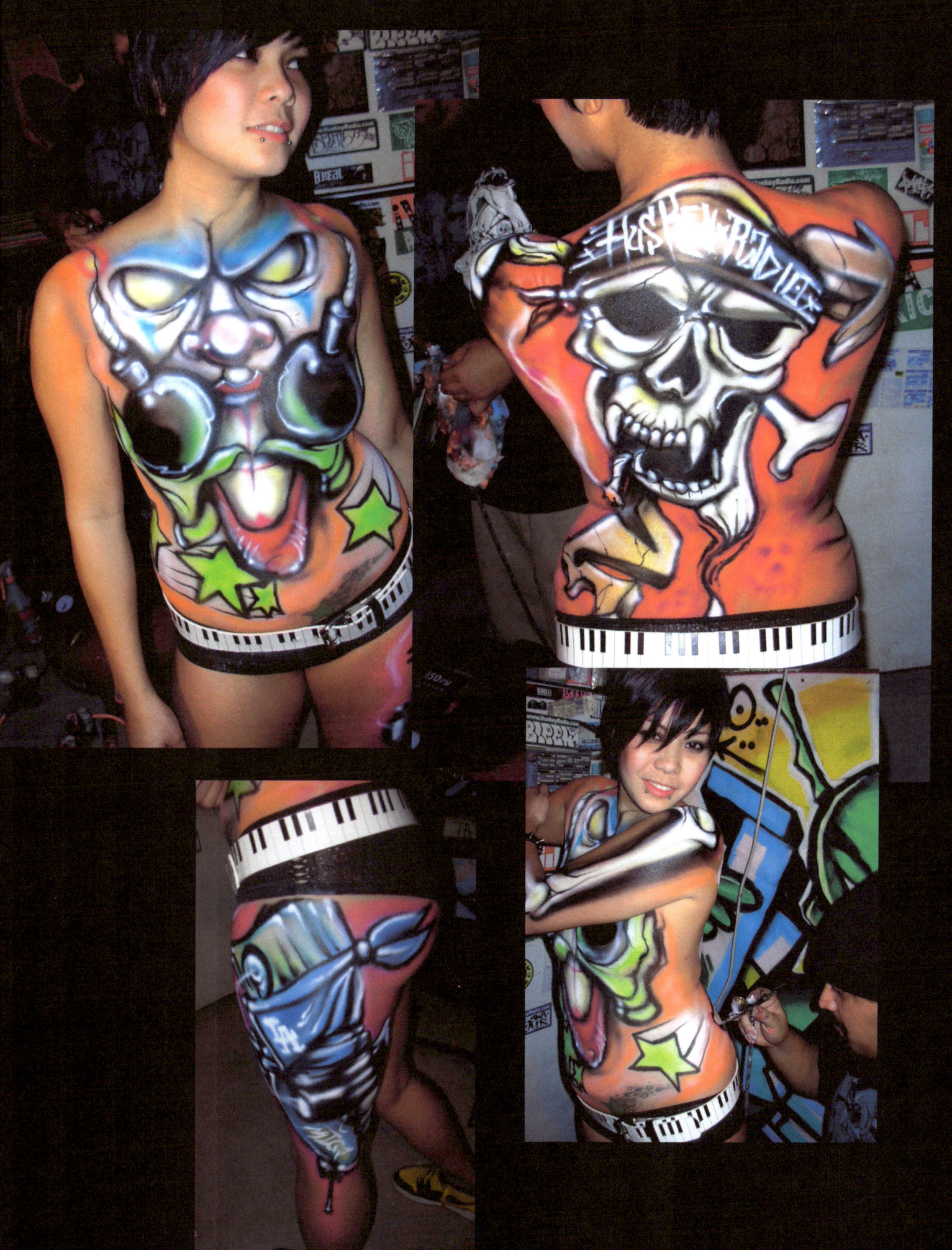

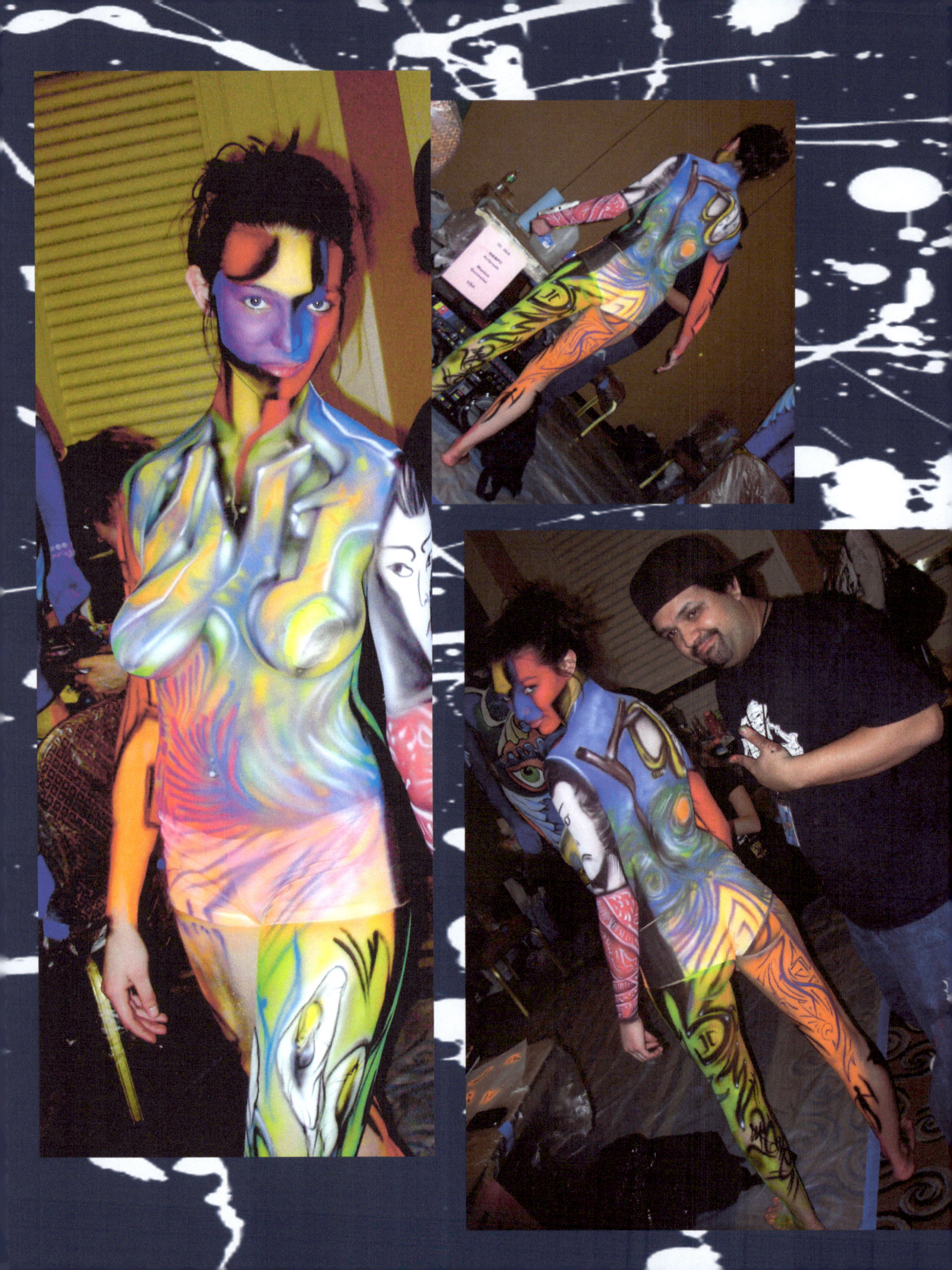

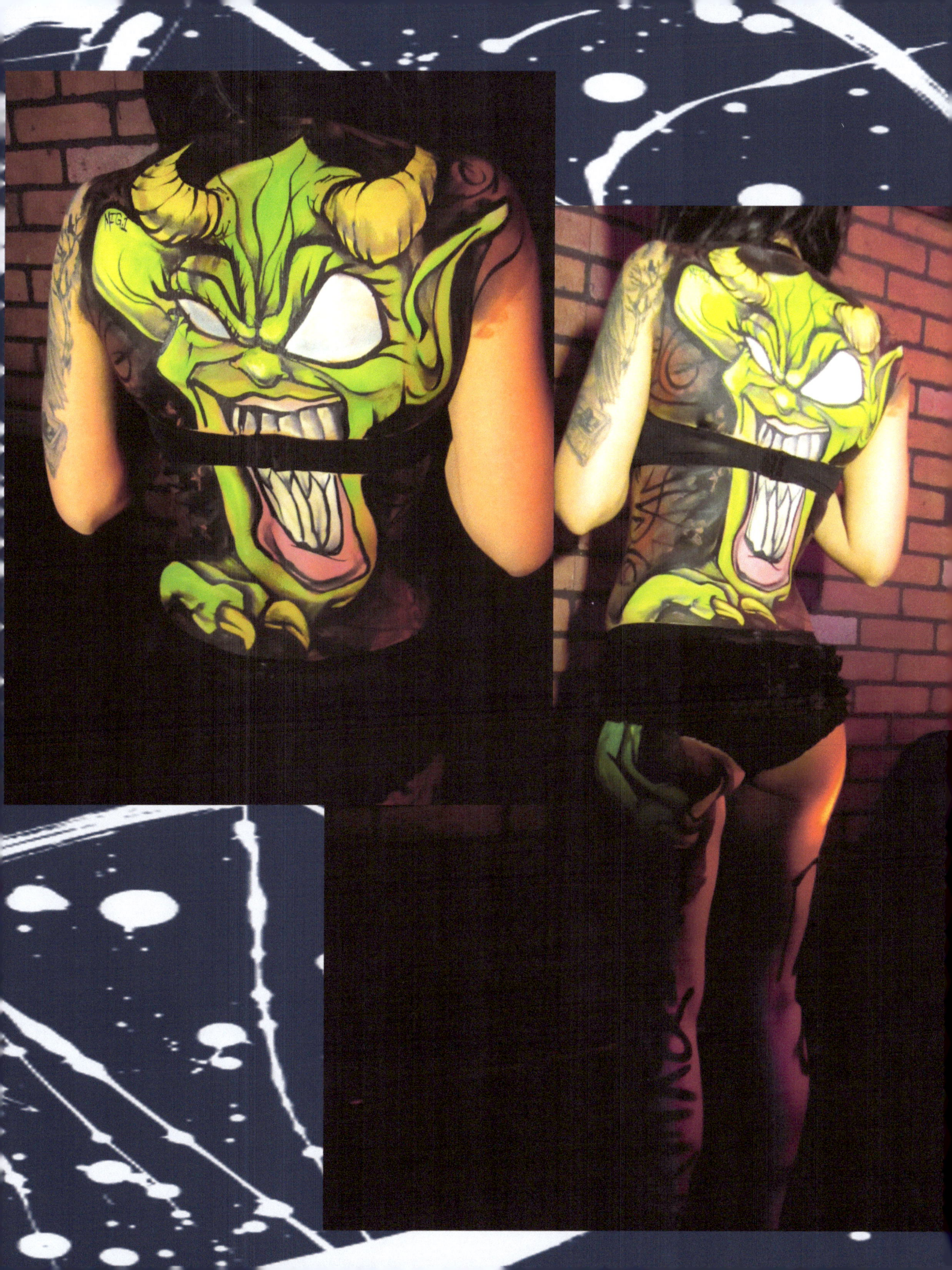

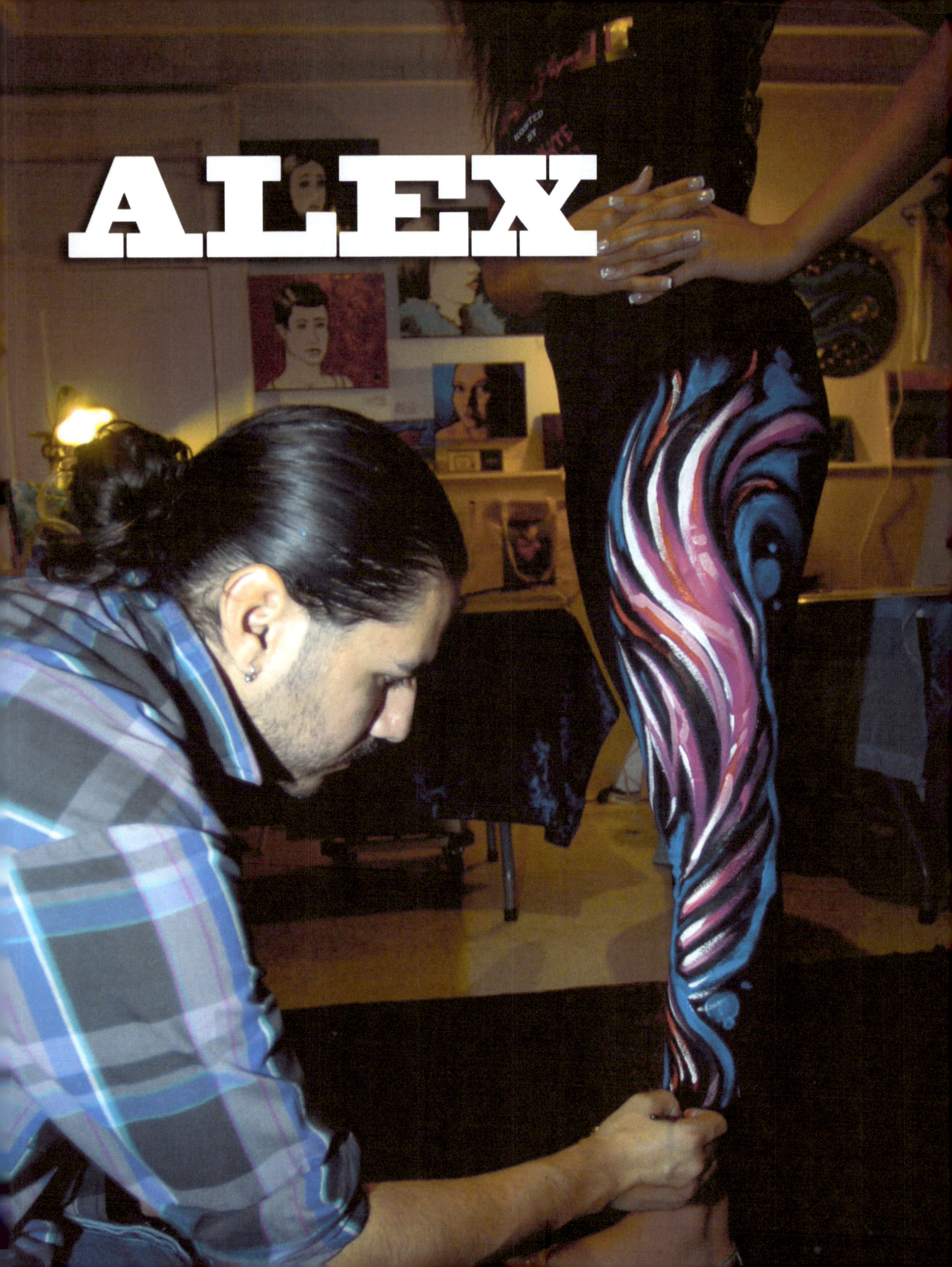

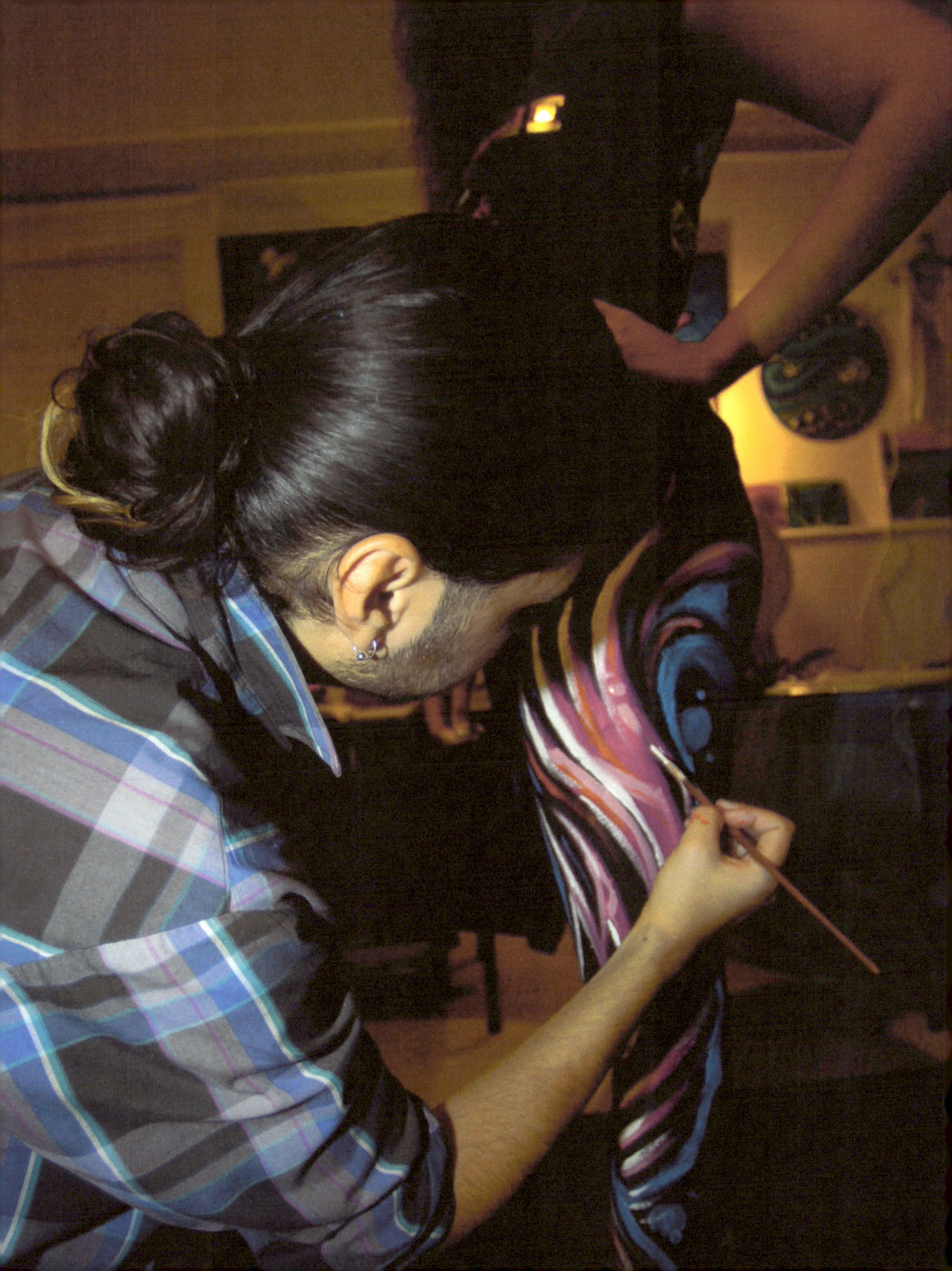

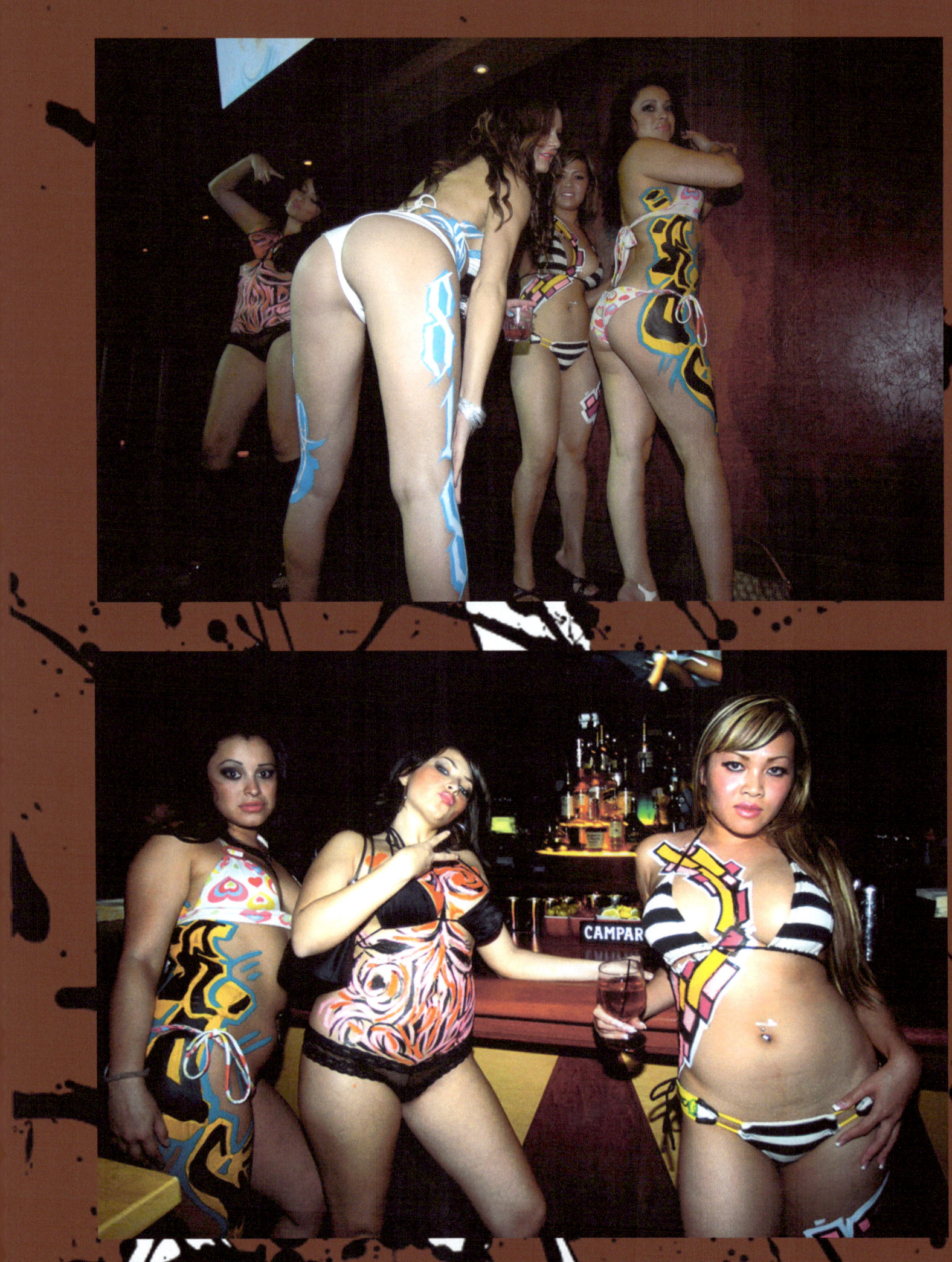

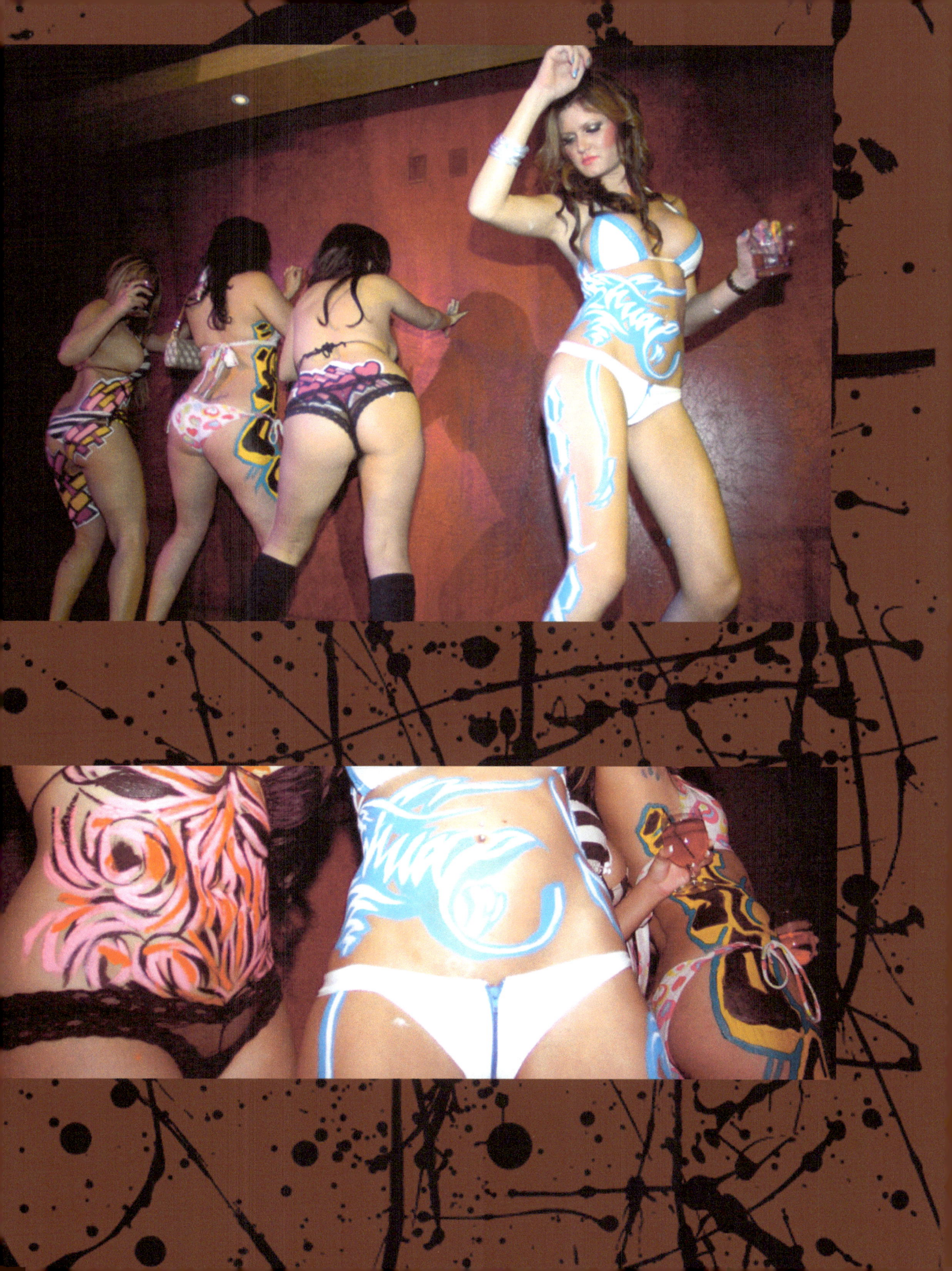

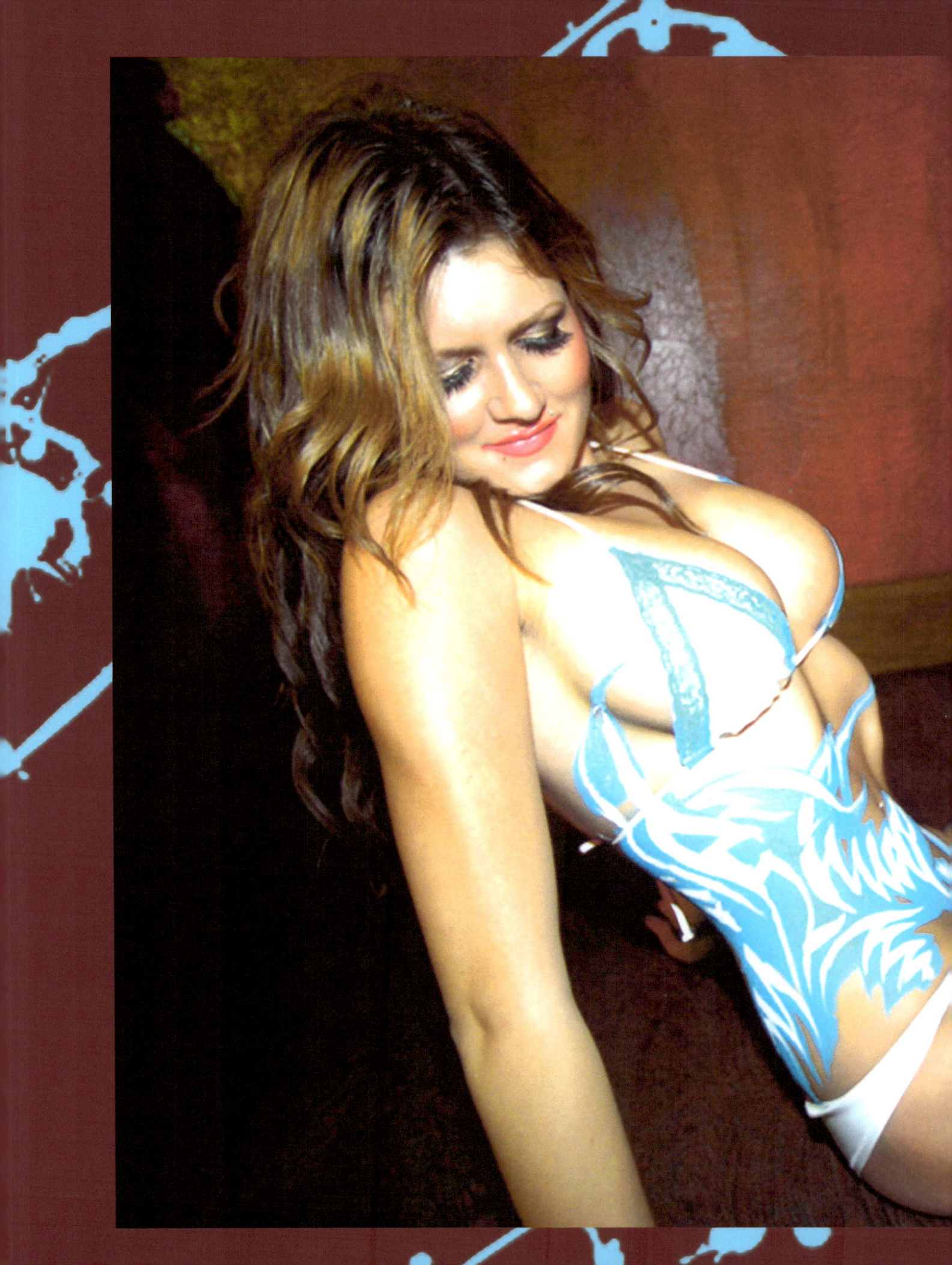

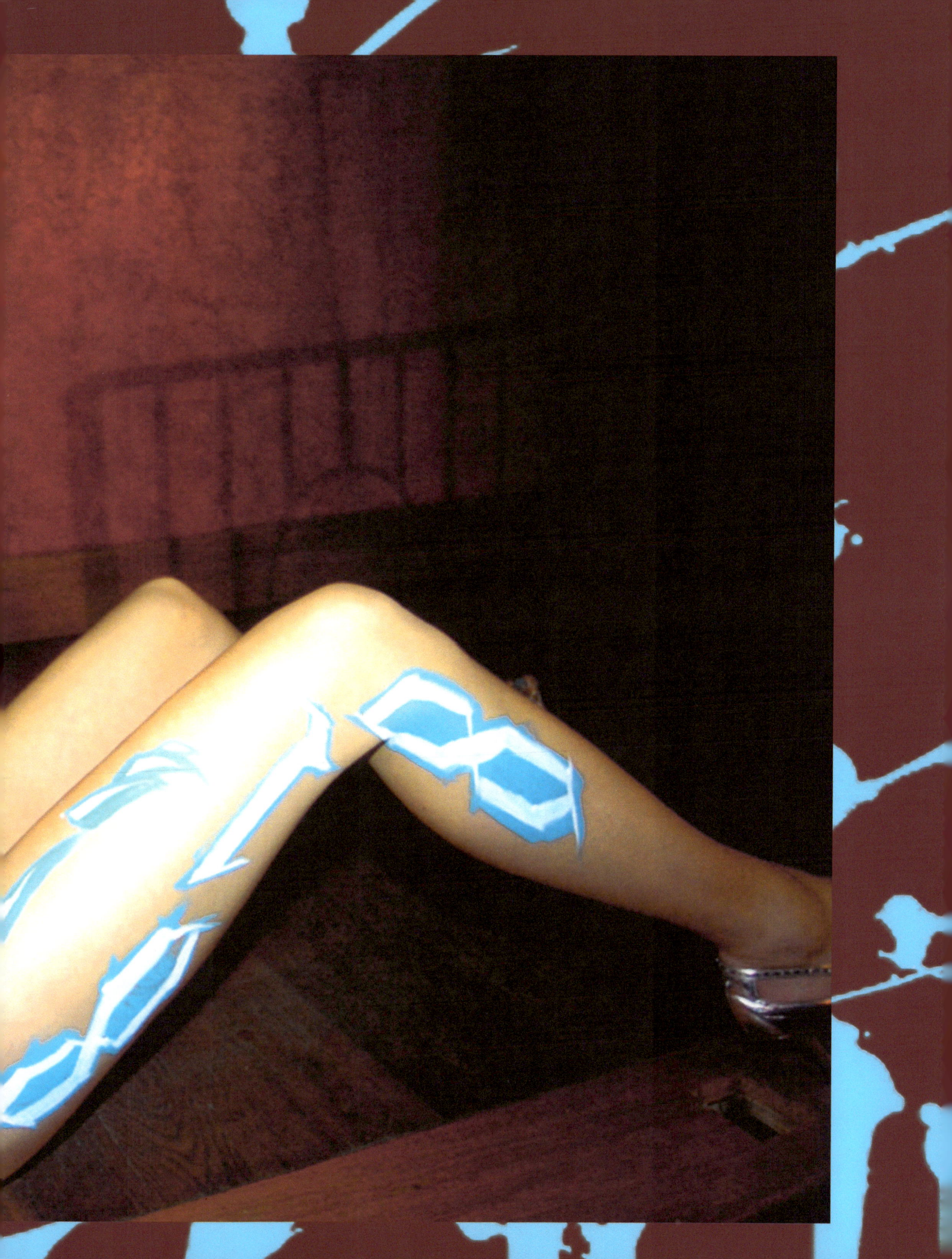

LIVE ON CAMERA MEDIA GROUP IS BASED OUT OF HOLLYWOOD CA. WE ARE THE ORTIZ SISTERS ARACELY AND ROSA ORTIZ, BORN & RAISED IN THE WEST SAN FERNANDO VALLEY. LIVING SO CLOSE TO HOLLYWOOD, WE HAVE ALWAYS BEEN INTO ENTERTAINMENT. WE ARE FOCUSING ON MAKING FEATURE FILMS, BUT WE LOVE DOCUMENTING EVERYTHING....HOPE YOU GUYS ENJOY THIS BODY PAINTING BOOK.
THE PICTURES REPRESENT A GATHERING OF WHAT WE LOVE!!!!! ARTIST, ART, CULTURE......

IG: LIVEONCAMERAMEDIAGROUP
FB: FACEBOOK.COM/LIVEONCAMERAMEDIAGROUP
YOUTUBE.COM/LIVEONCAMERA

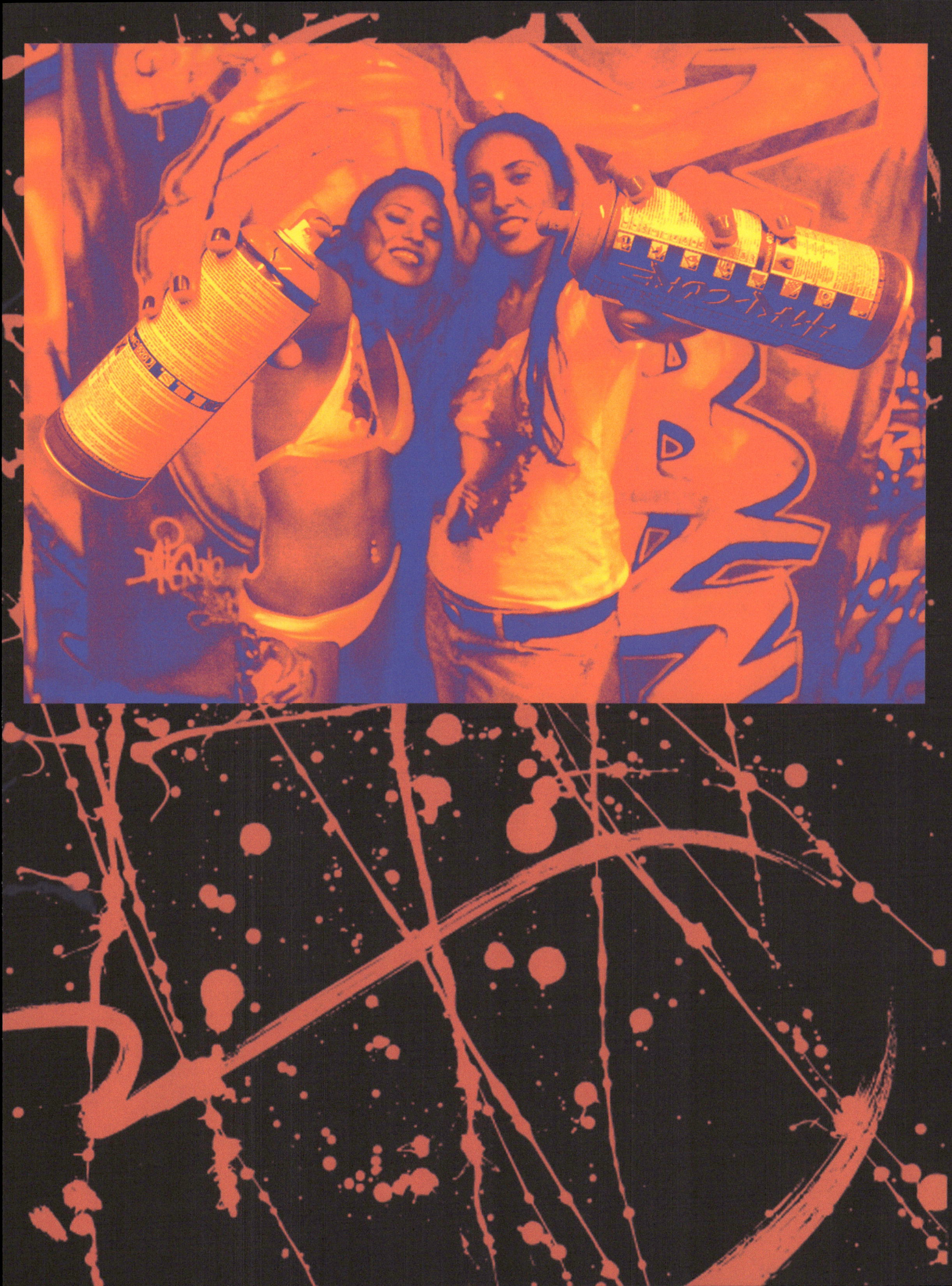

SPECIAL THANKS!

First, we would like to thank Paul Stewart at Over The Edge Books for this amazing opportunity to create a book of the pictures we have been gathering over the years. We would also like to thank all the amazing artists and the models for being a part of this project.

Migone: Thanks for working with us on putting the book together! We are really happy with how it came out!

ARTIST INDEX:

Page 1 - 10	BINHO	WWW.BINHORIBEIRO.COM.BR
Page 11 - 18	RISKEY	WWW.THAINKWELL.COM
Page 19 - 32	CHAZ	WWW.THECHAZMAN.COM
Page 33 - 36	EWOK	WWW.GRTV.TUMBLR.COM
Page 37 - 38	D.F	
Page 39 - 47	PESKY	Instagram: Pesky1er
Page 48 - 66	MIG ONE	Instagram: Migone2013
Page 67 - 72	ALEX	

MODELS INDEX:

Page 15, 16	Yvette Mendez	Instagram: @ibethom
Page 17, 18	Brandi Renee	Instagram: @missrenee10
Page 21 -22	Erika Reynolds	
Page 23	Sabrina, Tabitha Taylor	
Page 24	Marisa, Keanna Louise	
Page 25	Tabitha Taylor	
Page 26	Antonia Dorian	
Page 27	Nohea, Alisha, Marisa, Jacklyn, Desire	
Page 28	Tiffany	
Page 30	Mikey Lee	
Page 31	Natalie	
Page 37, 38	Suzie	
Page 47	Amber Cherry	Instagram: @cherry1_626
Page 49-52	Lola	
Page 57 - 59	Cali	
Page 53 - 54	Danielle M. & Heidi H.	
Page 57 - 59	Kallee B.	
Page 60	Tammy W.	
Page 71 -72	Candy	

PHOTOGRAPHER INDEX:

Page 11, 13, 14   FistHigh Productions   Instagram: @FISTHIGH

Page 12   Maurice Johnson   Instagram: @Moe_Jizzles

Page 15, 16, 49-52   Ricky Clay Email: PROFILMMAKER@AOL.COM

Page 21 - 32   Chaztography   WWW.THECHAZMAN.COM

Page 33 - 36   Gloria Parks

Page 37, 38, 43-46, 55-56 67, 68 Rosa Ortiz

Page 39-42, 47, 69-72 Aracely Ortiz

Page 53 - 54, 61 Cynthia Prod. By Sal - VADER BODY GRAFF

Page 57 60 Prod. By Sal - VADER BODY GRAFF

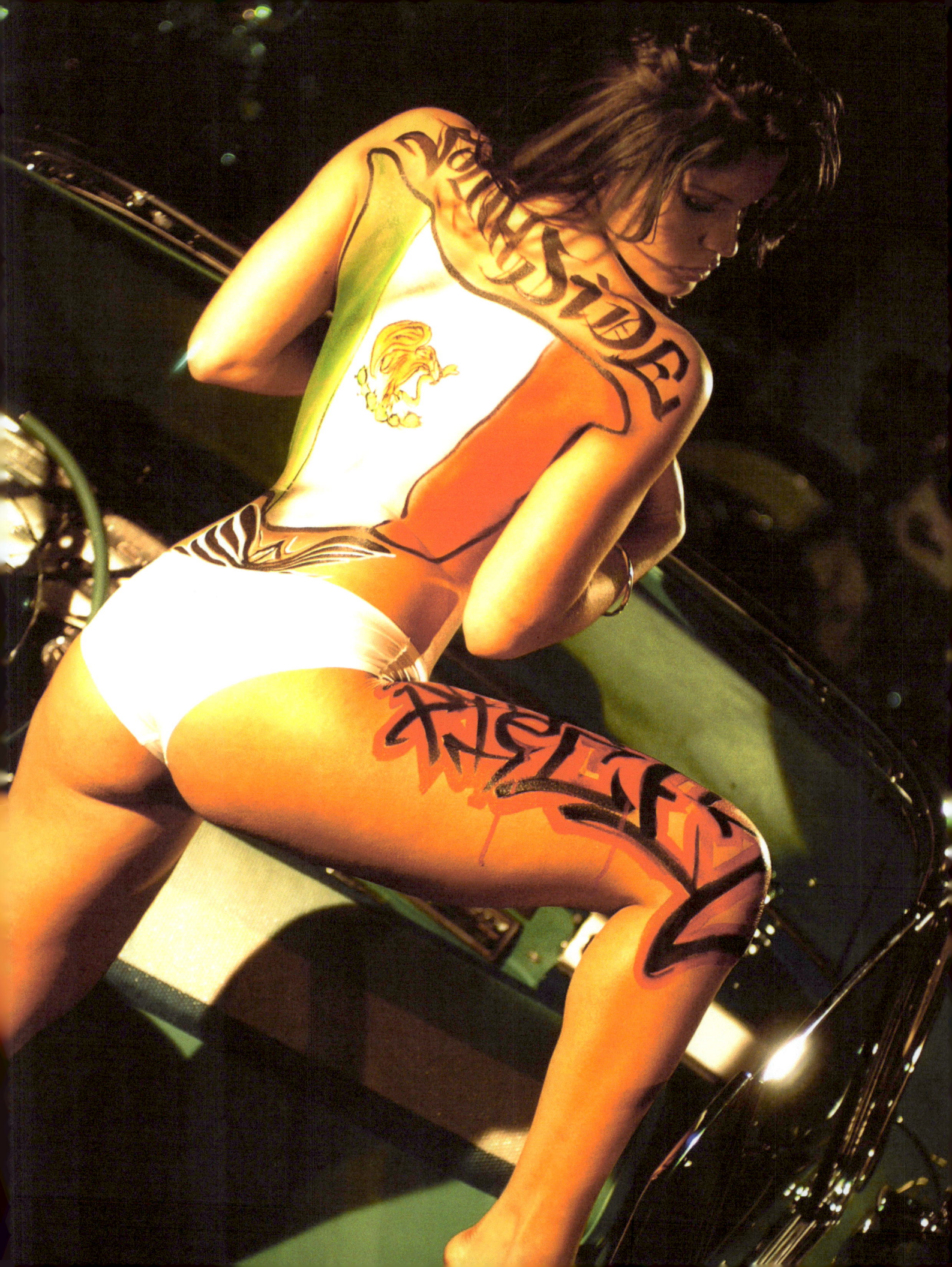